日本絵と

ILLUSTRATED
"SALARYMAN" IN JAPAN

[サラリーマン編]

ILLUSTRATED

"SALARYMAN" IN JAPAN

©**1996** by Japan Travel Bureau, Inc.
All rights reserved

1st edition·················Dec. 1986

7th edition·················Jan. 1996

Printed in Japan

About this Book

1) Layout

This book consists of the following six sections:
(1) A day of a Salaryman; (2) The life of a Salaryman; (3) The work of a Salaryman; (4) The lifestyle
of Salarymen; (5) The manners of Salarymen; (6)
Business related phrases and terminology.

You can read this book in any order you like. A
brief explanation refering to "Japanese management
and the salaryman" is attached at the end of this book
as an afterword.

2) Japanese Words

All the Japanese words in this book have been
romanized in accordance with the revised Hepburn
system. Except for the names of places and people,
all Japanese words are printed in italics except where
they appear in headings or bold type. Long vowels
are indicated by a line above, as in 'Shachō' and,
since e's are pronounced "ay" in Japanese, e's at the
ends of words are marked with an acute accent, as in
"shita-uké" (pronounced "shitahukay").

Dear Readers

● ●

This book focuses on the "salaryman," a special brand of worker unique to Japan. It is a historical fact that salarymen and the companies they work for have been the driving force behind the economic rise of postwar Japan. They have also garnered generous helpings of both praise and criticism from overseas sources in the process. All too often, however, these opinions are not based on fully accurate information.

In the pages ahead, enjoyable illustrations and easily read text are utilized to provide important insights into Japanese business society, concentrating on the mind and behavior of the salaryman.

For those tired of fragmentary or overintellectual reports of Japanese business, "SALARYMAN" IN JAPAN is for you. Take a stimulating journey into the practical work-a-day world of the salaryman – a journey guaranteed to deepen your understanding and enjoyment of Japan.

C·O·N·T·E·N·T·S

A DAY OF A SALARYMAN

THE LIFE OF A SALARYMAN

♨

THE WORK OF A SALARYMAN

THE LIFESTYLE OF SALARYMEN

A DAY OF A SALARYMAN
サラリーマンの一日

●

What are the daily realities of the salarymen who
supported Japan's Advanced economic growth.
How does their day begin and end?

THE SALARYMAN'S APPEARANCE

"Salaryman" is a word coined in Japan, used to refer to all white-collar workers who receive a salary. In a very real sense, salarymen are the driving force behind Japan's phenomenal postwar economic growth.

Metal frame, square-rimmed glasses.

Short hair parted at the side in the "seven-three" style.

Dark red necktie with diagonal stripes.

White cutter shirts

In the coat pocket: Address/schedule book, wallet, name card case, commuter train pass, etc.

Dark blue or gray suit.

Black leather shoes.

A Salaryman's Uniform

While a salaryman has no set uniform, there is a definite "unspoken code" which discourages the following dress.

Long hair and sunglasses are rarely seen, and even mustaches are frowned upon.

A white suit with loud open-collar shirt is considered "illegal" dress for a salaryman. Black suits are worn only for weddings or funerals, and businessmen decked out in yellow or red suits will have zero credibility.

The *kimono* is traditional Japanese dress, but has no place in a salaryman's activities. Someone like this would probably scare all the customers away.

Salarymen must refrain from following the latest hair styles or fashion trends.

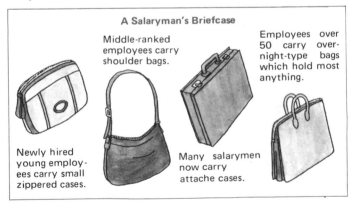

A Salaryman's Briefcase

Middle-ranked employees carry shoulder bags.

Employees over 50 carry overnight-type bags which hold most anything.

Newly hired young employees carry small zippered cases.

Many salarymen now carry attache cases.

● Kōin (Mr. Average Blue Collar)

Even if they receive a monthly salary, blue-collar workers are generally not known as "salarymen" (white-collar workers), but rather as *kōin* or plant workers. These workers don set uniforms before entering the plant, and their lifestyles differ considerably from their white-collar counterparts.

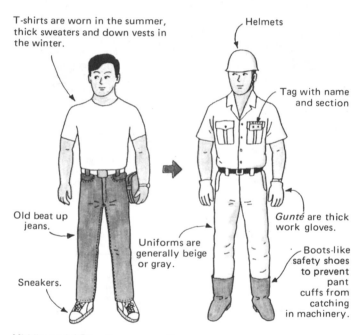

T-shirts are worn in the summer, thick sweaters and down vests in the winter.

Helmets

Tag with name and section

Old beat up jeans.

Gunté are thick work gloves.

Uniforms are generally beige or gray.

Boots-like safety shoes to prevent pant cuffs from catching in machinery.

Sneakers.

Middle-aged *kōin* often wear golf slacks and polo shirts. They will change to regular suits only after being promoted to management positions.

Kōin wear tags on their breast pockets with their name and section.

● OL (Office Lady)

"OL" is a term coined in Japan referring to all ladies employed in office situations. OL are generally hired between the ages of 18 and 22 and leave the company five to six years later to marry. Veteran female employees who go on to management positions are distinguished from OL as "career women."

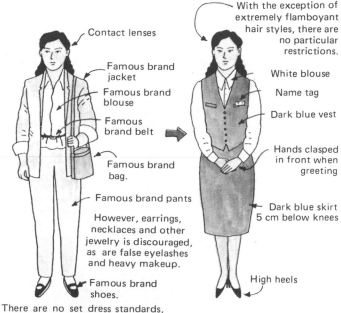

Contact lenses

Famous brand jacket

Famous brand blouse

Famous brand belt

Famous brand bag.

Famous brand pants

However, earrings, necklaces and other jewelry is discouraged, as are false eyelashes and heavy makeup.

Famous brand shoes.

There are no set dress standards, and OLs tend to choose popular fashions. However, wearing the same clothing two days in a row is taboo because it suggests staying out overnight.

With the exception of extremely flamboyant hair styles, there are no particular restrictions.

White blouse

Name tag

Dark blue vest

Hands clasped in front when greeting

Dark blue skirt 5 cm below knees

High heels

Uniforms vary widely by the type and personality of the company. Some mass media and apparel firms have no set uniforms.

● A Salaryman's Survival Kit

Alarm Clock

Digital alarm clock/ watches were popular, but now orthodox watches are the main trend.

Business Card (Meishi)

In Japan, no one does business without a *meishi*. (See page 58.)

Personal Seal (Hanko)

The *hanko* is used instead of the signature to validate contracts. (See page 74.)

Address/Schedule Book (Techō)

A pocket-size pad for jotting down schedules, addresses, phone numbers and other vital data.

Pocket Calculators (Dentaku)

Some are no larger than a credit card, powered by solar cells, and can store telephone numbers and other information.

Pocket Pager (Poketto Beru)

Almost all salesmen carry pocket pagers. The beeping noise of these units can often be heard in trains, coffee shops, movie theaters or other public places.

Wallet and Purse (Saifu)

Small change is vital for making phone calls, riding trains and other needs. Many of these needs may now be covered with special cards.

Credit Cards

Though cash remains to be the mainstream payment method, credit cards have become quite popular.

Bank Cards

In a metropolis the size of Tokyo, banks can be found on most of every street corner. There is little need to carry large amounts of cash around.

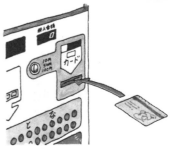

Telephone Card

Can be used in green phone booths.

Orange Card

Can be used at orange-colored Japan Railway ticket machine for convenient "cashless" ticket purchases.

THE SALARYMAN'S MORNING

■ The Salaryman

6:30 a.m.
The typical urban salaryman lives in the suburbs, an average of one to two hours by train from his office. His day thus begins extremely early in the morning.

6:45 a.m.
He is generally half asleep as he shaves and brushes his teeth.

■ Plant Worker

6:30 a.m.
Plant workers normally live close to their factories, and can sleep later in the morning.

7:30 a.m.
The plant worker is still dreaming.

16

Raw egg

Broiled fish

Fried eggs

Toast

Rice

Miso soup

Coffee

The Typical Salaryman's Breakfast

7:00 a.m.
He doesn't have time to waste and bolts his breakfast as he scans the newspaper.

7:15 a.m.
When particularly pressed for time, he will devour a slice of toast as he dashes out the door.

8:00 a.m.
Plant workers walk or bicycle to work.

8:30 a.m.
About the time the salaryman reaches his office the plants are starting up. Plants usually begin work between 8:00 and 8:30 a.m., head offices and trading companies between 9:00 and 9:30 a.m.

COMMUTING

Commuting is a very trying time of the day for Japanese salarymen. In Tokyo, nearly 10 million people head for the same general business district during the same hours each day. Sometimes this creates a tremendous rush hour crush.

Ropes are stretched across the top of stairways to limit the number of passengers on the platform at any one time.

Oshiya ("pushers") are part-time help who shove passengers into the packed train so the doors can be closed.

Riders are bumped and swayed in packed trains for an hour or more.

By the time the typical salaryman arrives at work, he has already expended a good portion of his energy reserve for the day.

● Surviving Rush Hour Commuter Trains

Keep your arms as high as possible, to avoid being mistaken for a molester!

Guard against pickpockets by not carrying your wallet in your back pocket.

Don't lose your temper if someone steps on your toes. You may tramp on his foot at the next lurch of the train.

Don't resist the swaying of the train, just roll with the flow. This is the safest, most comfortable way to ride.

Be careful when you put something in the overhead rack. You may not be able to reach it when you have to get off!

● How to Pass Train Time

The salaryman goes to great lengths to pass the time spent on packed trains.

Typical Commuting Patterns by Age Group

Comic books targeting junior high students.

Music favorites are young female idols or American pops.

Sports newspapers

The young salaryman uses a portable cassette tape recorder to enjoy music while reading comic books.

The middle-aged salaryman reads newspapers, weekly news magazines or paperback books. Sports newspapers are particularly popular and report on baseball and other sports and recreation.

How to Read a Newspaper on Packed Trains

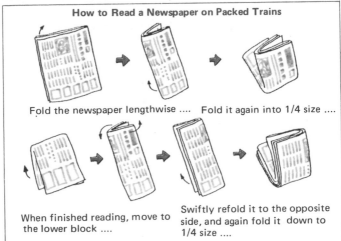

Fold the newspaper lengthwise .... Fold it again into 1/4 size ....

When finished reading, move to the lower block ....

Swiftly refold it to the opposite side, and again fold it down to 1/4 size ....

● Other Modes of Commuting

In one corner of the lot is a pile of stolen and discarded bikes.

Roads are very congested during commuting hours, making the bus impractical. Most salarymen ride to the nearest station by bicycle.

Special bicycle parking lots are provided to prevent the station area from being overrun.

Almost all plant workers commute by car. The plants are located in the suburbs, making it only about a ten-minute ride.

Salarymen driving cars to the office will sometimes only advance about 300 meters in ten minutes.

MORNING GATHERINGS

Morning gatherings are conducted regularly by specific work groups daily or on specified dates. The group leader gives a short speech, followed by announcements of that day's (or week's) suggestions, decisions, objectives and other key areas by those in charge.

Morning gatherings are conducted in different ways by different industries. One of the most extreme approaches is found in the sales sector.

Morning gatherings for salesmen resemble taking the field for battle.

At plants, safe work practices are confirmed.

Big trading companies rarely hold morning gatherings, while employees drink coffee or look over newspapers on their own.

At department stores and other retailers, customer service manners are reviewed.

RADIO CALISTHENICS

Warming up calisthenics are performed for about 10 minutes along with music from the radio or by group chants *(Rajio Taisō)*. Most plant employees participate in this routine before starting work.

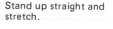

Stand up straight and stretch.

Bend from right to left.

Swing arms from right to left.

Spread out arms and breathe deeply.

Bend to the rear.

Bend over forward to stretch.

Naturally, plant work is rarely rigorous enough to truly require warming up. Like the morning assembly, the main goal is to boost worker spirit and morale for the day ahead.

LUNCH TIME

A salaryman's lunch hour is from noon to 1:00 p.m. Here's how they spend it:

Most eat lunch at nearby restaurants. There are large crowds at lunchtime, and popular restaurants sometimes require a 20-minutes wait.

Plant workers normally eat lunch at employee cafeterias. The food is cheap but not always so tasty.

Tachigui soba (noodles eaten while standing) enjoys vast popularity among salarymen. Located at train stations and on street corners, these counter noodle shops offer quick and cheap meals.

Newlywed salarymen bring an *aisai bentō* ("devoted wife box lunch") from home.

● Lunchtime Entertainment

OL compare boyfriends or how they spent their weekends.

Salarymen talk about work, naturally.

Some OLs eat their *bentō* (box lunches) in parks or on the company roof, and chat with their co-workers. Some also enjoy volleyball or other noontime recreation.

Salarymen sit and talk in coffee shops, or go for a short jog.

At plants, some workers play catch or other light sports at nearby fields.

Some return to the office immediately after eating to resume work.

OVERTIME

Almost all companies require overtime work (after 6:00 p.m.) on a regular basis. Some employees put in as much as 100 hours of overtime a month, meaning they spend the majority of their time at the company.

10:00 p.m.
To keep from nodding off, workers will drink coffee or tea. If that doesn't work, some resort to pep-up tonics made from snake skin extract and other exotic ingredients.

7:00 p.m.
During overtime, meals will often be catered from nearby restaurants to eat at the office. Typical choices are *rāmen* and other Chinese food, *katsudon* (pork cutlet on rice), *tendon* (shrimp *tempura* on rice) and other *tenyamono* (catered dishes).

1:00 a.m.
When a salaryman misses the final train home because of overtime duty, he has a choice of grabbing a cab or staying in a hotel. Some choose to pass the night on an office sofa.

HOLIDAY WORK

Like overtime, there are occasions when the Japanese business-man has no choice but to work on a holiday. Although the number of companies adapting to a five day work week has in-creased, there are still salarymen who cannot devote their weekends to personal pursuits.

8:00 a.m.

Salarymen who work on holidays find themselves on the same train with young people or families off on weekend outings.

12:00 a.m.

The restaurants in business dis-tricts are closed on holidays, forcing many salarymen to eat fast food.

8:00 p.m.

If the work load is particularly heavy, they end up staying at the office well into the evening hours.

11:00 p.m.

There are also times when late-night work on holidays is deman-ded. By the time he gets home everyone has already turned in, and once again he fails to see his own family.

A SALARYMAN'S NIGHT LIFE

Intense work schedules expose salarymen to considerable stress. To relieve this tension, many go out drinking at night.

The words and a film showing images of the song add to the atmosphere.

Middle-aged salarymen are particularly fond of such bars, and there are some who own *karaoké* sets to polish their skills at home.

The songs most widely sung in *karaoké* bars are *enka*, a popular form of Japanese ballad.

Customers rarely pay attention to performances by others.

Particularly popular are *karaoké* "snacks" or bars. *Karaoké* is an abbreviation for "empty" (*kara*) "orchestra" (*oké*) and refers to crooning into a microphone along with taped musical accompaniment.

Snacks and bars are very popular with salarymen, who rarely drink with anyone but their own colleagues. Complaints or frustrations about superiors or subordinates dominate the conversations.

Sometimes salarymen return home so tipsy they can't walk straight. To avoid being chastised by their wives, they carry home a snack or other small present as a peace offering.

Younger salarymen and OLs tend to prefer discos or French restaurants.

Then again, some salarymen go right home from the office to catch up on their work, study computer programming, law or whatever.

BUSINESS IN JAPAN

What is business in Japan? If we compare it to business in other countries, we find differences everyone ponders over. Japanese business is successful today, so others wish to find the formula to Japanese business and use this same formula as some magic incantation.

Yet, what is business? People is the answer. If business in Japan is successful, it is because of the Japanese people, the result of Japanese civilization. The qualities and disadvantages of business are but a reflection of a country's social organization and its people.

Therefore, if we speak of the efficiency of Japanese business, we find it is partly due to the over-staffing as compared to Western business. But, mainly, it is sustained by the devotion of the people working together to the group, to the company, to the Japanese society. They become the cogs of the company machinery or, the members of one big family, the enterprise.

These characteristics are at the antipodes of business, French-style, where lack of discipline and antagonisms between individuals as well as the conflict of interest between employee and company are handicaps but are also the consequence of the inividualistic, contentious spirit of the French that includes more creatively. In Japan, business problems are mainly due to the social principles of "no disturbance" and "team spirit" that lead to little constructive communication and expression of individual ideas, and eventually to a lack of dynamics.

Much could be said on the way a people's characteristics affect business within a country. But the main point to be aware of is how much a part of a country's culture business can be.

Virginie Noël (France) Journalist

THE LIFE OF A SALARYMAN
サラリーマンの一生

●

In Japan, the company comprises a large
portion of the salaryman's life. Their lives are condensed
into the approximate 40 years from the time they
join a company until retirement.

JOB HUNTING

Over 70 percent of salarymen are college graduates. Their efforts to secure employment have become ritualistic, with particular rules and customs followed. Almost all salarymen remain with the same company through retirement, making initial employment a crucial event with a major impact on the rest of their lives.

Tense face

White cutter shirt

Dark blue suit.

Sometimes the price tag is still attached to suit.

The proper hairstyle is the short, seven-three part "recruit cut."

Dark red necktie.

Instead of a briefcase, an envelope containing explanatory materials about the company visited.

Pants pressed.

Black leather shoes.

"Recruit Style" College Students

The so-called "recruit style" is considered the orthodox fashion for jobseekers or new salarymen. Those dressed any other way will be considered nonconformists and will lose points in the scramble for jobs. "Recruit" is a company which specializes in information for young people in search of their first employer or those wishing to change jobs. The word "recruit" has become widely used in this context as a result.

● Job-hunting Activities

The job-hunting season is limited by a mutual pact between companies to prevent early recruitment from undermining fair employment activities. Nevertheless, the official starting date is not always honored.

There are days when visits to prospective companies are not permitted. Large numbers of students are dressed in the orthodox "recruit style" of clothing.

An outline of the company, as well as the qualities and skills they are seeking from prospective employees, are presented during the explanatory meeting.

Afterwards a notice is sent out and an interview is held.

Next, a written exam is administered. An informal letter of acceptance is finally issued.

Companies naturally want to hire the best candidates and use various methods to initiate contacts before the official green light. This practice is known as *aotagai* (buying before the harvest), meaning to buy the rice while it is still green in the field.

Alumni representatives take him out to dinner to sell him on their company.

The company offers further persuasion through university professors.

The interview stage exam, the written exam, and a board interview is then held.

Receives an acceptance notice from the company and stops job-hunting.

The company begins to keep watch to see that he doesn't sign up with anyone else. Time after time he is treated to lavish meals.

The company takes him off to a resort to halt any ideas of further job-hunting.

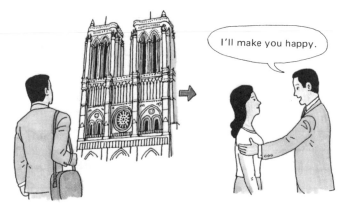

I'll make you happy.

There are some students who leave on an overseas trip after having decided on a company.

Finds a gorgeous, intelligent girl-**friend and begins to dream of the** good life ahead.

Finding a job is a major step in life. College students begin preparations for this process in their senior year, and those who over-enjoy during this time may find it difficult to be accepted by a good company. Some choose to repeat their senior year to prepare for the hiring tests the following year.

Goes out drinking with his friends every night, paying little heed to the future.

Spends most of his time with his steady girl.

Becomes absorbed in mountain climbing, swimming, tennis or other sports.

While almost all his classmates have landed jobs, he is still searching for leads in newspapers and magazines. At this point, however, there are few if any attractive jobs left over.

The Changing Employment Structure in Japan

Along with the changes in Japan's industrial structure, there is increasing growth in secondary and service industries. The service sector, for example, accounts for approximately 60 % of the total new workforce.

Japan's population is ageing and so is the average age of its workers. This has triggered projections of a collapse in the working population pyramid, which could result in insufficient social security capital and promotion positions from here on. Some 56% of Japan's workforce is over 60 years old, the highest level of any nation in the world.

There is a steady rise in the academic background of new employees, a reflection of the increasing advance to high school and college, not to mention the demand for higher educated personnel to respond to today's rapid technological innovation.

Higher education, the lower birth rate, greater leisure time and other factors have led to greater social participation and will to work among Japanese women. Female employment has roughly tripled over the past two decades. In April 1986, legislation calling for equal employment opportunity for men and women was passed in Japan.

NEW EMPLOYEE EDUCATION

New employee education is designed to teach new workers basic knowledge about the company, as well as how to behave as responsible adults. Some companies adopt extremely unique education methods.

Eat together.

Sleep together.

Play together.

Study together.

Cooperation

One popular method of teaching cooperation is the training camp *(gasshuku)* experience. Groups of salarymen retreat to mountain lodges or temples, where they lead extremely disciplined lives for a set period of time.

Kekkafuza style

Eyes half-open.

Sit up straight.

Lock thumbs

Place left palm over the right.

Place right leg over the left.

Spiritual Strength

Zazen (Zen Buddhist meditation) is practiced to cultivate the spirit.

Physical Strength

Jogging, *jūdō*, *kendō* or other sports are used to build the physical strength demanded of salarymen.

Door-to-Door Sales

Trainees make sales calls without prior appointments. Often, they call on 100 customers without making a single sale!

In businesses which demand considerable customer contact, new employees are put through rigorous training in bowing and other types of greetings, speaking, telephone manners, smiling and other behavior techniques. Some companies bring in educational experts, or consign this program to firms specializing in new employee training.

OJT

On-the-job training is widely used, with trainees assigned difficult but educational jobs.

SALARY

Normally, basic salary *(Kyūryō)* is determined by age and educational background. Consecutive service at the same company assures a steady rise in salary, and few salarymen consider moving to other firms.

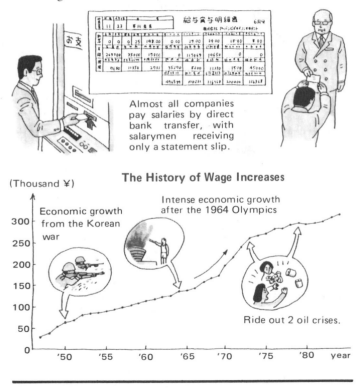

Almost all companies pay salaries by direct bank transfer, with salarymen receiving only a statement slip.

The History of Wage Increases

(Thousand ¥)

Economic growth from the Korean war

Intense economic growth after the 1964 Olympics

Ride out 2 oil crises.

40

● Bonus

Bonuses are generally paid twice a year, in June and December. Some companies pay bonuses at the end of their fiscal periods. Bonuses are rarely based on individual merit but represent a set percentage of the base salary.

Rank-and-file salaryman

Bonuses are also paid by bank transfer. In the past, however, the rule was to pay the cash in an envelope, with position assessed by whether the envelope stood up or not.

Executive salaryman

A salaryman's bonus is engulfed by the following:

Home or car loans

Children's schooling

Ochūgen and *oseibo*

(see p. 120)

Family trips during summer and New Year's holidays

Wife's clothes

SENIORITY SYSTEM

Nenkō-joretsu is a seniority system in which a salaryman's position rises in direct proportion to his age. This system has survived largely on the strength of support from labor unions. It is also considered an effective method to heighten company loyalty and establish family-oriented management. However, modern-minded managers are now edging toward the merit system so widely practiced in the United States and Europe.

While all salarymen start out equal, all cannot be promoted. The company prepares a wide range of vague titles for salarymen who have somehow drifted off the "elite course."

Almost there....
Almost there ....

Ahh, still so far to go ....

I'm going to the top!

The seniority system is rooted in modern Japanese philosophy and Confucian beliefs, which equate importance with a person's age. In traditional Japanese companies, very few salarymen have subordinates older than them.

More Japanese women have attained management posts than ever before. These women easily outwork run-of-mill men and are usually very good at what they do. Sex discrimination has been legally banned at all jobsites in Japan.

The "elite course" refers to steady promotion to executive status along the most direct route. Salarymen can generally judge their ultimate rank in the company by the speed of their promotions. As a result, almost all realize how far up the ladder they can rise several years after being employed.

Only salarymen who have compiled broad experience in various different areas will rise to positions of true importance. In short, no one skyrockets into a top management post overnight, no matter how talented they may be.

COMPANY QUALIFICATIONS

Most Japanese companies also have in-house qualification systems *(Shanai Shikaku)*, with proficiency tests offered for computer skills, foreign language and other areas. Such qualifications are a definite advantage in ascending the corporate ladder, and salarymen study hard to improve themselves.

Mr. Elite

6:00 p.m.

Mr. Normal

8:00 p.m.

1:00 a.m.

An "elite salaryman" works from 8:00 a.m. to 8:00 p.m., then studies from 9:00 p.m. to 1:00 a.m.

Stopping off for a drink or two naturally delays a salaryman's return home. He may find his way to the doorstep, but his furious wife has locked him out!

Computers are used throughout Japanese industry, and more middle and advanced-age managers are learning how to use them.

Seeing how proficient young subordinates are with computers can be a real shock.

Shock turns to panic after attending a computer course and not understanding a word.

Even hiring a personal computer tutor doesn't help.

Eventually, all confidence fades, followed by a nervous breakdown.

MIDDLE MANAGEMENT

A crucial step in the career of a salaryman is the advance from a *hira* (rank-and-file worker) to a management position. Lower middle management is perhaps the least enviable stage in this process, as such managers must endure complaints from both above and below.

I must be the most miserable man on earth!

Unreasonable demands from superiors.

Home loans.

Selfish requests from subordinates.

Rebellious sons.

The cost of bringing up children.

Fun-loving daughters.

Cheating wives.

● Elite Employee Education

Middle managers at Japanese companies are noted for their diligence and dedication. There are companies which specialize in 'manager cultivation education.' Let's examine what type of programs they offer....

To test patience and endurance, sudden assignment to door-to-door sales along with new employees.

To test mental and physical strength, standing under a waterfall or in the ocean at winter.

To test the ability to deal with adversity, mountain survival programs.

Salarymen who have completed manager training courses return to the company in a new frame of mind.

TRANSFERS

A salaryman employed by a company with many branches will normally be transferred several times as his career advances *(Tenkin)*. Where, and to what position he is assigned, is a pivotal career concern.

Promotion **Demotion**

Eiten (Promotion Transfer)

Assignment to a higher position in a branch in a major city is a clear promotion. Co-workers and subordinates gather to congratulate him before he departs for his new assignment. Salarymen are naturally attracted to a superior who may be able to improve their own status in the company.

Sasen (Demotion Transfer)

Assignment to a small regional branch, even in a higher position, is considered a strong sign of *sasen* (demotion). In this case, only a few truly close friends see him off. In principle, however, a change of assignment is considered a promotion.

• Tanshin-Funin (Solo Assignment)

Solo assignment (*tanshin-funin*) is a unique transfer format in which a salaryman is assigned to a branch office away from his family. There are various reasons for living alone, one being the focus on children in Japanese family relations and the concern that a superior education will not be attained in the prefectures. Businessmen who refuse to go on solo assignment are literally discarding their hopes of career advance.

The husband must do his own cooking and laundry, often a lonely and aggravating experience.

Only on payday does the wife remember that, yes, she is still married.

A considerate husband tries to come home on weekends, with most of his own pocket money used to pay the transportation costs.

Less considerate husbands just send home the money, creating an atmosphere which increasingly resembles divorce.

SWITCHING JOBS

In Japan, switching jobs requires a high degree of commitment on the part of the individual. Since almost all companies in Japan assume the employee will remain there throughout his entire career, it is extremely difficult to switch from one company to another.

Scouted by a headhunter, he joins a new company.

Searching for a means to use his own abilities, he quits the company.

His abilities land him in an executive post at the new company, too.

However, he ends up being ignored at the new company too.

There are still few instances of being vaulted into an executive position through the help of headhunting firms which operate widely in the U.S. and Europe.

Close human ties develop in Japanese companies, with salarymen entering from other companies often shunned as "outsiders." This is particularly true of someone from a competing corporate group.

脱サラ

GIVING UP THE SALARYMAN LIFE

A *datsusara* is someone who quits the company to set up his own business. Most salarymen dream of becoming a *datsusara* sometime during their career, but with success stories few and far between, only a handful ever make the move.

Two Types of Datsusara

Goodbye youth....

The Ambitious Datsusara

This type gives up being a salaryman to launch his own company. He gathers together people who's abilities have gone unrecognized by their companies and moves to pioneer new business. This type often underestimates the role of the big company in his success to date and fails when he attempts to strike out solely on the strength of his own reputation.

The "Retired" Datsusara

This type wasn't cut out for the salaryman life from the start and leaves to run a coffee shop or *penshon* (small resort lodge) to farm or adopt some other lifestyle he has always dreamed of. Naturally, this is rarely an easy road either.

TEMPORARY TRANSFERS

Temporary transfers (*shukkō*) occur for the purposes of loaning out an employee to work in an enterprise associated with his place of employment.

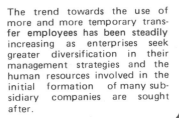

The trend towards the use of more and more temporary transfer employees has been steadily increasing as enterprises seek greater diversification in their management strategies and the human resources involved in the initial formation of many subsidiary companies are sought after.

Since there is an obvious difference in the scale of operations between a subsidiary company and the main firm, those temporary transfers who come from the ranks of basic management are accorded a degree of treatment in the subsidiary company usually reserved only for those in a higher level position.

Those temporary transfers who come from the mid level positions in the company are often able to return to higher level posts in their main company after they have scored a considerable number of solid achievements and gained sufficient experience in the transfer assignments.

There are also many cases of older transfer employees who, having previously retired from the company, are completely absorbed into the subsidiary company as full members.

Many employees quite familiar with various kinds of practical merchandise information from their day to day dealings with customers often are sent out on transfer assignments. These kinds of knowledge gathered in department stores, boutiques and other shops dealing with the latest trends and fashions serve as the basis for the temporary transfers to the manufacturers that supply these various companies.

Many competent employees of a smaller size enterprise who possess special technical abilities often come into a large scale company through a transfer position. Once they are successful, they may stay with the new venture in the position of a scout for other valuable sources of technical ability.

RETIREMENT

Most salarymen retire between the age of 55 and 65, having worked at the same company for some two-thirds of their lives. This marks retirement a major, often traumatic event. In short, they must come to grips with the unknown experience of "not going to the office."

Ideally, a salaryman will be warmly congratulated by his subordinates at this time, and proceeds to retire into leisure, surrounded by his children and grandchildren.

He retires from his company at the mandatory age and is re-employed at a smaller firm.
While the salary is lower, he is stimulated by the entirely new work environment.

After retirement, many people take up different types of work to give their life new meaning in their golden years.

Those previously unable to follow personal pursuits now have the time to immerse themselves in a wide range of hobbies such as painting, calligraphy, dancing, etc.

The number of retirees who want to stay in good health by keeping on the move has reached new heights with many involved in softball, croquet, orienteering and other popular sports.

There are others who are more than happy to have another opportunity to study in an informal community college type of learning environment. Some will even set out to write their autobiography or memoirs.

Recently, large numbers of elderly couples have taken to traveling on long, leisurely trips to various locations.

THE AD BUSINESS
AND SALARYMEN

The advertising business in Japan is prosperous and the large companies can expect a 10% growing rate for the coming years. This is an area where the internaionalization of business can be best seen. Japan manufacturers sell their products all over the world and to sell they need the support of sales and promotion materials. In this way, the large Japanese advertising agencies comes to be a cross road for the whole world. For this reason, this business and the men involved in it show a less pronounced Japanese stereotype. They are more open minded and cosmopolitan. Nevertheless, when we come to talk about the structure of the companies itself, the relationships between its members and the way of dealing and securing a client, the advertising conglomerates don't differ much from the rest of the Japanese corporations. A western manager would probably change many aspects of their vertical structure and organization and follow a different business approach, but this would be, in many senses, like willing to change the very same fact that they are Japanese. In any case, the high technology developments are coming one after the other, and Japan and the Japanese are changing their way of doing business, their attitude towards the world and their own lifestyles. And they are changing fast.

Daniel Monteverde (Argentina) Copy writer

THE WORK OF A SALARYMAN
サラリーマンの仕事

●

What is Japanese style business?
Let's look at this mysterious, yet in one sense
successful, system of business.

NAME CARD OR BUSINESS CARD

A salaryman's business card *(Meishi)* contains his company's name, address and telephone number, and his own name and official title. Business cards are an extremely important tool because they testify to the owner's identity. Someone without a card will be dismissed as a business entity no matter how capable they may be.

The title on the name card is the single most important factor in judging a salaryman's business worth.

A company's reputation will often be judged by its address. Companies located in major office districts in the center of Tokyo, where land prices are sky high, tend to be highly evaluated, while those in the suburbs, residential areas or entertainment districts are not looked upon so favorably.

東菱鋼機株式会社

管理本部 営業室

課長

田中三郎

〒101 東京都中央区日本橋本町一丁目一番一号
電話（〇三）九九九一 九九九一（六六代表）
内線九九九九番

One standard of reliability is whether a company owns its **own building** or simply rents office space.

Two phone numbers, one for the main switchboard and the other for the salaryman's own desk, will create an impression of a large company.

● How to Use The Business Card

> I'm Saburō Tanaka, pleased to meet you.

> Saburō Tanaka ....

The salaryman in a relatively lower position will present his business card first. Proper protocol requires that he states only his company and his own last name and not his title.

The card is received with a bow, with time taken to read the company name, title and individual name. A business card is considered an extension of its owner, and should be treated with respect.

> I got it. Now I can put the card away.

> Shall we get started?

After memorizing the person's name, place the business card in the *meishi* case. When many people are present, the cards may be placed face up on the table, but this is not really recommended.

Only when these steps have been completed will both parties be seated and begin business talks.

● How to Treat the Business Card

To bend or damage the business card in front of its owner is a direct insult.

The owner's name and title should be memorized. Retrieving the card to reconfirm the owner's name is extremely poor etiquette.

Most business cards are blank on the reverse side, offering convenient space for jotting down memos. But this is also taboo.

When the card collection becomes unmanageable, it should be placed in a holder. This is far easier than making an address file, and over the years the personal history of a salaryman can be gleaned from a look into his name card file.

Name cards have such high credibility that crooks can sometimes commit fraud using someone else's card. To guard against this, **when handing out cards, police** officials or high-ranking bureaucrats often write the name of the person it was given to and date on the back.

Meishi can also act as a substitute to one's actual physical presence. If a person one visits is not in, one will leave their *meishi* as a substitution and leave.

Types of Salarymen Disliked in Japan

A poll surveying types one would not like to work with had "people who break promises" at the top of the list. The Japanese place a high value on verbal promises. Those who do not keep their word soon find themselves with few, if any, business contacts.

Those who break promises

Those who don't pay their debts.

Those with bad drinking habits

Those who talk too much

肩書き
TITLE

Japanese companies contain many different posts. The distribution of authority varies from company to company, making it very difficult to tell how much power a salaryman has simply by looking at his name card *(Katagaki)*.

**Kachō-hosa
(Assistant Section Manager)**

The post directly beneath section manager.

Kakarichō (Chief Clerk)

The most common post for a salaryman around the age of 30, with authority over a small section. The title of *kakarichō* in one's late 20s is a sign of an elite salaryman, but for someone over 40 it could indicate removal from the elite course.

Hira (Rank-and-File)

Hira refers to the lowest rank of salaryman, who has no title on his name card. Most are in their 20s, and although some have titles such as *shunin* (chief) all are ranked fundamentally the same.

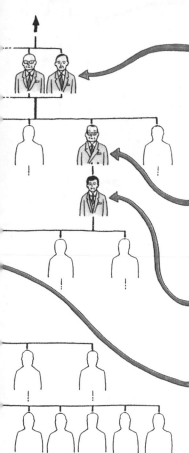

Torishimariyaku (Director)

Only upon becoming a *tori-shimariyaku* a salaryman will truly become part of the company's top management. This post is divided into two classes: *Hira-torishimariyaku* (normal director), and *Jōmu-torishimariyaku* (executive director) or *semmu-torishimariyaku* (managing director).

Buchō (Department Manager)

A salaryman is generally considered among the elite if he becomes a *buchō*. However, there are some *buchō* who have no subordinates.

Jichō (Assistant Department Manager)

The post directly beneath department manager. Only about one of 10 salarymen will ever reach this level.

Kachō (Section Manager)

From *kakarichō* to *kachō* is known as middle-management, and represents the most demanding ground for salarymen. The future executives of most companies become *kachō* in their 30s.

Kaichō (Chairman)

An honorary position appointed to a retired president. Although not involved in actual day to day affairs of the business, his authority is equal to that of the president since he is involved in key decision making matters.

Sōdan-yaku (Advisor)

Japanese companies have a custom of looking after their executives for the rest of their lives. *Sōdan-yaku* is an honorary post for retired *kaichō* or main shareholders, although, as with the *kaichō*, there are some companies in which *sōdan-yaku* possess extensive business authority.

Komon (Counselor)

Fundamentally the same as *sōdan-yaku*, an honorary post generally reserved for retired directors.

Shachō (President)

Normally, a president rises through the posts of director and vice-president. The president is nominally the top man in the company.

Kansayaku (Auditor)

An executive in charge of accounting. In many companies this post is equal to the rank of director.

Kōjōchō (Plant Manager)

The man in charge of a single plant, corresponding to a *buchō* in a normal company.

Shitenchō (Branch Manager)

The manager of a bank branch or other office. Managers of larger branches correspond to *buchō*, while those of smaller branches are closer to *jichō*.

Hombuchō (Headquarters Manager)

The position of headquarters chief defines the role of one in charge of several departments or in certain cases the central figure of authority for an organization. This position found in some of the larger companies is established at the executive level or just one step below it.

Shitsuchō (Office Chief)

The leader of comparatively a work unit smaller. A post equal to that of a normal section chief, although a "president's office chief" may possess considerable authority.

APPOINTMENT

Naturally, an appointment is needed to meet for business talks. Salarymen normally make their appointments by phone.

> Hello, I'd like to speak to XX in the management division.

One method is to send an inquiry by mail, and then phone up to check out the results. This is often used for making appointments at government offices.

When calling, it is critical to ask for the person in charge. At Japanese companies, vague inquiries are often cut off at the switchboard, making it important to know the name and position of the person you need to contact.

Sudden calls without an appointment are known as "*tobikomi eigyō*" (jump-in sales) and are successful only around 10 percent of the time.

● The Most Effective Methods

A purchasing supervisor at a large company receives dozens of phone calls daily and most are not accepted. To meet such a supervisor, it is necessary to devise an effective plan of attack.

Salesmen from overseas companies can improve their chances of meeting the man in charge if they carry a letter of introduction from an embassy or government body.

Trading company

To interest a Japanese company in importing, the best approach is to work through a trading company. An experienced manager from such a firm will handle all the necessary arrangements.

Another method is to receive an introduction from someone in the company. This is particularly effective if the introducer ranks above the supervisor.

Some salesmen resort to using private connections to get an appointment. Parents and other relatives are all fair game, and at times elementary school teachers or other persons will be pressed for introductions.

● Honné and Tatemaé (Real Intention and Principle)

The difference between *honné* and *tatemaé* can genuinely baffle overseas salesmen. This refers to the difference between what one says and what one thinks. It is not an attempt to deceive the other party, and most business talks *(Shōdan)* proceed with the understanding that this fine boundary is understood.

In Japanese, "*hai*" does not mean "yes." It should be understood as an assurance that "I do hear what you are saying" and nothing more.

To grasp someone's real intentions, it is vital to keep track of their every word and gesture.

A smile can contain a light sense of denial and should not always be accepted at face value.

The Japanese avoid direct expression of their *honné*, using various signs to convey it. Only experience will cultivate understanding of this process.

● Nemawashi (Laying the Groundwork)

Very rarely will a business talk result in an on-the-spot decision. Important matters will lead to more talks, delaying the final decision. *Nemawashi* refers to the method of completing this lengthy process before the actual business talk. It is normally conducted in the following manner:

First, an unofficial meeting is held with the manager in charge, to present the issue and request *nemawashi*.

The manager talks with those (with decision-making authority) who will attend the final conference and gains their unofficial approval.

An official business talk then takes place, with the company formally deciding to study the matter.

The conference is held with those present offering official approval. In this way, the decision is reached much sooner than through the normal process.

IN-HOUSE DOCUMENTS

Communication through documents which clearly state their message and can be easily stored is a crucial consideration within Japanese companies. A common example is the *ringi* (circulation) system, in which a proposal is passed up the company ranks, receiving stamps of approval from each person involved. Typical examples of in-house documents include:

Shimatsusho (Written account)

Apology and explanation of the circumstances when a work rule has been violated.

Shintai-ukagai (Informal resignation)

Submitted (to his superior) by a salaryman who has caused a major loss to the company, to assume personal responsibility for the incident.

Kikaku-sho or Ritsuan-sho (Plans & Proposals)

New job plans, proposals and other ideas are normally submitted to superiors in writing. Many companies also provide creative proposal systems, in which ideas may be deposited in boxes.

Shutchō hōkokusho (Business trip report)

A report detailing customer calls, time spent, and areas discussed during a business trip.

BUSINESS TRIPS

Business trips *(Shutchō)* are very common in Japan and are especially frequent between Tokyo and Osaka, the nation's two economic centers. In the near future, use of new media in business exchanges is expected to reduce the volume of unnecessary travel.

"Round-trip"trips between Tokyo and Osaka by the Shinkansen bullet train (three hours each way) in the same day are far from unusual.

"Capsule hotels" are a new concept, providing "capsulized" sleeping space at a low price.

"Business hotels" in larger cities cater to salarymen on overnight business trips, offering a simple room which may include breakfast the next morning.

Salarymen are expected to bring their co-workers souvenirs (usually local delicacies) from at least one out of three trips.

In an attempt to eliminate wasteful travel, some companies have introduced television conference systems.

CONFERENCE

Because of the emphasis on group decisions, Japanese companies hold lots of conferences *(Kaigi)*. Two conferences a day, or over 10 per week, is not at all rare. There would be no problem if these conferences were efficient, but in many cases the result is major time losses.

In their 20s, salarymen work hard to study the conference content and strive to articulate their own views.

Salarymen who are too busy or swamped with their own work become distracted during meetings, pondering other business problems.

Middle managers sit back and pretend to take notes at conferences which do not directly concern their own duties.

Nearing their 50s, managers may doze off in the midst of heated discussions.

A well-known Japanese manager believes that "conferences should be conducted standing up." His point is that such meetings need to be more efficient to avoid wasting time.

Seating arrangements for meetings are predetermined.
It is common to have the *Gichō* (the chairman) sit first, and then proceed according to rank, with those in the higher positions sitting first.

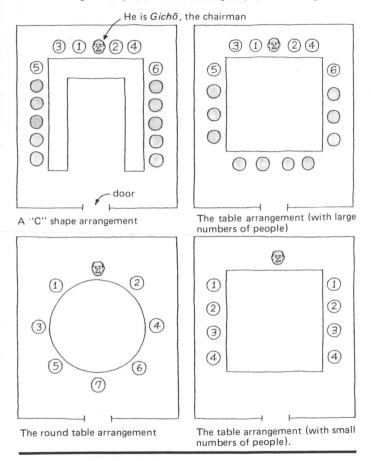

He is *Gichō*, the chairman

A "C" shape arrangement

The table arrangement (with large numbers of people)

The round table arrangement

The table arrangement (with small numbers of people).

PERSONAL SEAL

Instead of signatures, Japanese use personal seals (stamps) engraved with their name. This is also called using a *hanko*. Contracts are invalid without such seals, and to live and work in Japan it is vital to understand the use of the *inkan*.

Three major types of *inkan* are generally used: *Maruin*, *kakuin* and *ginkōin*.

Maruin (round seal)

The seal of the company representative, usually round in shape and about 18mm in diameter. The *maruin* is used to formalize contracts.

Kakuin (square seal)

The seal with the company's name used for various reasons although possessing little binding legal authority. Contracts sealed with the *kakuin* but not the *maruin* are sometimes declared invalid.

An *inkan* is used to deliver an official seal to public offices, which will issue notarized certificates of this seal upon demand. Business offers are normally accompanied by official documents with notarized seals.

Other stamps widely used at companies include the following:

Shinten ("Confidential")

Relatively important documents are put in an envelop, which is inscribed with the name of the intended recipient and stamped "Confidential." Naturally, only the person designated is supposed to open it.

Maruhi ("Secret")

This seal means the document must not be taken outside the office or copied without special permission.

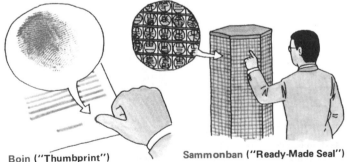

Boin ("Thumbprint")

When one is not carrying the personal seal, the thumbprint of the right hand may be used. But strictly speaking, it is not accepted in business matters.

Sammonban ("Ready-Made Seal")

The *inkan* must be specially made to serve their purpose as the signature. *Sammonban* are cheap, massproduced *inkan* for use on documents of limited importance.

● Special Uses for Inkan

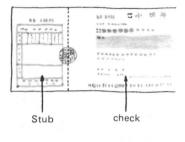

Stub   check

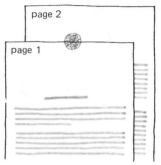

page 2

page 1

Wariin (tally seal)

Affixing a seal over the edges of two or more copies of the same document, to verify that they are identical.

Keiin (joint seal)

Affixing a seal over the edges of all pages in a single document, to verify the sequence.

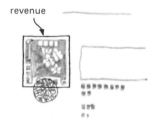

revenue

Keshiin (cancellation seal)

Special tax revenue stamps must be attached to contracts, receipts, or other documents exceeding set values. The *keshiin* is affixed to these stamps to prevent their recycled use.

Teiseiin (correction seal)

Affixed to the revised and deleted sections of contracts which are corrected, to verify that the revisions were not added illicitly later on.

Sutein (contingency seal)

An extra seal added to sanction further revision ahead of the time. This can be quite convenient because the *inkan* need not be affixed again even if mistakes are found or revisions made. However, it can also open the door to illicit use and is only recommended when the recipient of the sealed contract can be fully trusted.

Tomein ("the end" seal)

Affixed at the end of a contract to verify the conclusion. Another seal which can provide the opportunity for illicit use.

Mekuraban ("blindman's seal")

Automatically stamping documents without reading them, it's a method widely used by workers who must process huge amounts of relatively unimportant documents.

Sain (signature)

Many Japanese believe that no contract is valid without an *inkan*. However, the signature is also an acceptable means of closing an agreement. In fact, simply the *inkan* with no name may be declared invalid at times. It should also be remembered that the *inkan* may be affixed over either a signature or a typed name.

CHECKS AND NOTES

Checks and notes are widely used in Japanese business as well. However, use patterns differ from those in the West, making knowledge of a few basic points important.

● **Kogitté (Checks)**

There are eight areas to examine when receiving a check. If all are not in order, it will be impossible to cash the check.

— Is the payment amount clearly recorded?
— Does it contain the name of the payer (bank name)?
— Does it contain the payment place (address of the bank)?
— Does it contain the date of payment?

— Does it contain the location of issue?
— Does it contain the signature or registered seal of the payer?
— Does it contain the date of issue?
— Does the check bear the sentence: "Please pay the holder the above amount in exchange for this check"?

To avoid amount tampering, the written value must contain the yen sign (¥) on the left and an asterick (*) or star (☆) on the right.

Sembiki-kogitté ("crossed checks") containing two horizontal lines on the upper right are paid through the payee's bank account, guarding against loss or theft.

● Tegata (Note)

There are *yakusoku-tegata* (promissory notes) and *kawase-tegata* (bills of exchange), while the former type is most common. There are eight points that should be run when receiving a *tegata*.

Is the payment amount clearly recorded?
Does it contain the name of the payee (or payee's company)?
Does it say "promissory note?"
Does it contain the date and place of issue?

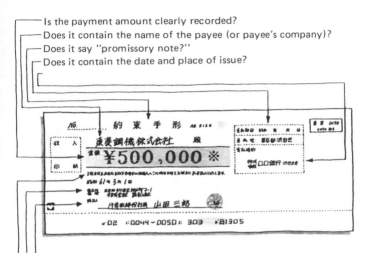

Does it contain the signature or registered seal of the payer?
Does it contain the place and address of payment?
Does it contain the sentence "The above amount will be paid to you or a designated party in exchange for this note"?

Notes which have been received may be substituted in place of **cash payments by affixing one's** registered seal on the back. This is known as *uragaki* (endorsement).

Cashing in such a note at a bank before the date of maturity is known as *waribiki* ("discounting"). An amount corresponding to the interest through maturity will be deducted.

RECEPTION

In principal, business transactions are between companies, although the actual decisions are made by the individuals in charge. This leads naturally to entertainment of those in pivotal positions, to strengthen relations and curry favor in receiving contracts.

The most common form of *settai* is the use of "clubs." Ginza, still Tokyo's most exclusive entertainment district, contains dozens of luxurious clubs. Most customers who drink at these establishments are known as *shayōzoku* ("the expense-account crowd"), because they are there on company money.

The hostesses at these clubs familiarize themselves with regular executive and *shayōzoku* salesman customers and tailor their services to a customer's specific work and temperament.

Another leading *settai* is golf. The cost of playing at Japanese golf courses is extremely high, making a round at a famous course on a holiday an effective means of impressing a client.

Mahjong is also widely used for customer entertainment. Such games often require the skill of "losing gracefully" to one's opponent. If the client loses big he will naturally become frustrated, while if wins big he may grow tired of playing. A happy medium is advisable.

Salesmen must first learn the hobbies and tastes of the managers they approach. When competing with companies on the same basic footing, this knowledge will contribute to more effective entertainment measures.

Company A learns that the manager likes to golf and treats him to takes him to a leading "night club."

Company B learns that the manager likes to go out drinking and a round on a famous links.

However, the manager awards the contract to Company C, where his brother is employed.

OL'S DUTIES

Whereas OL were once involved primarily in serving tea and making copies, the times are changing. With the passage of equal opportunity legislation in Japan, the number of women in pursuit of specialized jobs (and not general office work) is on the rise. There are more female managers than ever before, and this trend is certainly expected to continue.

Newly hired female employees are put in charge of serving tea and coffee *(ochakumi)*. However, with more and more companies installing automatic coffee makers, there is less and less need for such *ochakumi*.

Copy-making *(kopī-tori)* is another job once assigned solely to OL. But the advance in office automation has enabled anyone to make large volumes of copies in a flash. As a result, this monotonous chore is no longer assigned exclusively to OL.

Some OL only enter a company to kill time until they marry and will resign as soon as they find their man. This trend is also changing, however, and many OL stay on the job even after taking their nuptial vows.

Many women devote themselves to professional careers. To them, maintaining harmony between home and office can be a major burden.

OLs perform many other roles within the office as well.

OL are fond of gossipping in the kitchen area. These exchanges often reveal extremely accurate views of the work attitudes of co-workers and relations with superiors, providing an important source of in-house information.

Experienced OL are able to size up a visitor's importance immediately and know whether or not to serve tea. New employees can learn much about customers from observing such women in action.

OL can also teach new recruits much about how to generate fluid human relations and other fundamentals in becoming an accomplished salaryman.

OL who marry salarymen serve to further cement the bonds between the company and its employees.

SPIRIT OF COMPANY LOYALTY

One of the key secrets behind the strength of big Japanese companies is employee loyalty. These companies take good care of their people, and the belief in repaying this support with firm loyalty is deep-rooted.

Shakun (Corporate Articles)

The *shakun* is much like a constitution. The details differ by company, although most concern mental or spiritual attitude. At some companies, employees recite the *shakun* during the morning gatherings (*chōrei*).

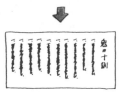

Shaka (Company Song)

The *shaka* is the company anthem. It is sung at New Year's Parties (*shinnenkai*) or other company events.

Shashō (Employee Badge)

The *shashō* is a badge worn on the lapel and corresponds to a military squad ID patch. Wearing this badge enforces a sense of belonging to the company.

● Shanai Gyōji (Company Events)

Official in-house events used to help orchestrate employees include the *nyūsha-shiki* (hiring ceremony) and *shinnenkai* (New Year's party).

Nyūsha-shiki (Hiring Ceremony)

A gathering held each April to welcome all new employees hired from the new fiscal year. The president urges all recruits to become effective employees and responsible members of society, with everyone then singing the company song.

Shinnenkai (New Year's Party)

A gathering held on the first day of work after New Year's to pray for renewed prosperity. The president gives a speech, everyone sings the company song, and a toast is held after the traditional *banzai* cheer.

I'm from _____ company. My name is _____.

Participating in this process, young salarymen soon learn to state the company's name before their own when meeting new people.

As his company loyalty is strengthened, the salaryman comes to regard the company as his father, his lover, his child, even his god. Such a salaryman will devote body and soul for the company's sake.

LABOR UNION

With the family-oriented nature of Japanese companies, labor unions cooperate with the management in protecting overall company interests, avoiding large-scale strikes in most cases (*Shuntō*). However, because the wage scale for the new fiscal year is determined in April, spring will often bring transportation and other strikes. The collective bargaining process adopted during this season is known as *shuntō*, literally, the "spring offensive."

Labor union and management representatives meet to discuss wage increases. This is a familiar scene in Japan each spring.

May 1 is the "May Day" festival for workers. Employees from nationwide industrial unions gather to express political slogans and engage in other activities. In recent years, however, a picnic mood has come to dominate these gatherings.

Although transit strikes have diminished considerably in recent years, whenever they occur, employees commuting long distances to the company resort to all sorts of methods to make it to work.

Commuters converge on the limited number of train stations in service, creating massive confusion.

Driving to work will drag on late into the afternoon.

Exasperated, many walk along the tracks toward the city center.

Some pack their suits into ruck sacks and bicycle to work.

During strikes, since local hotels are soon booked up, some workers must spend the night in the office.

There is a trend among some workers to use all of their paid vacation to spend more time with their families and get away from the drudgery of work. This has been labeled the "new family" phenomenon.

SALARYMAN TYPES AND CATEGORIES

● **Classification by External Appearance**

Far more applicable than blood typing. But, be careful! There are plenty of exceptions!

Rank-and-File Type

The unmarried rank-and-file salaryman enjoys the most easygoing lifestyle. He has no responsibilities either at work or at home and wears a relaxed, easygoing expression.

Middle-Management Type

This is the most demanding period in a salaryman's career — at work, at home, and financially. He wears a harried expression and has no time to worry about fashion or other non-essential concerns.

Executive Type

Brimming with confidence from winning out in the salaryman survival game, he puts on a little roll around the middle, and his cheeks swell out. He is also a little thin on top and wears a soft, relaxed expression.

Researcher Type

This type delivers the impression of being quiet, serious, even rustic. He is good at his job but much less skillful at socializing. Many in this category come from scientific or engineering backgrounds.

● Generational differences in Salaryman

Below are a list of the negative aspects of salarymen by generation.

(1) The 60's "The burnout Syndrome" Moetsuki Shōkōgun

It is an illness seen in the middle aged salarymen who, having devoted themselves entirely to their work, supported Japan's growing economy. Upon reaching the *Kachō* level, they immediately burnout.

(2) The 50's "The Workaholics" Mōretsu Shain

Without so much as a glance back at their families, they live for their work only. The company is the battlefield for them, for which they will use any means available to achieve their goals.

(3) The 40's "The In-between Years" Dankai-no-sedai

Born during the babyboom years, they are now caught in the middle between the older established generation and the young. Their student years were spent as radicals, though they now are concerned with their families, something which they are receiving heavy criticism for.

(4) The 20's "The Newcomers" Shin-jinrui

They are the generation that does not know war. They are an enigma to the older generations, who have no idea how or what they think. Their values and logic appear totally foreign.

● Three Types of Managers

Company managers are often compared to famous Japanese warlords. There are three major examples used.

The Tokugawa Ieyasu Type

Tokugawa is the great general who founded the *Edo* shogunate, a government which stayed in power for over two and a half centuries. He was a man who waited patiently for the right chance. An old comic *haiku* expresses this type in the following verse.
The silent bush warbler.
Let us wait
Until it sings.

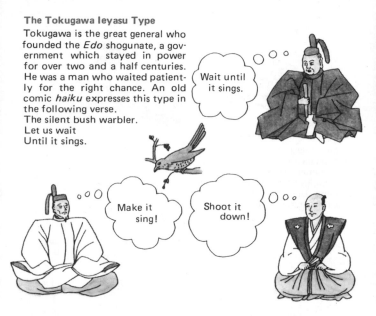

The Toyotomi Hideyoshi Type

Toyotomi was a brilliant ruler who brought a new political system to Japan. He believed strongly in his own abilities and dealt with all challenges in a firm and positive manner.
The silent bush warbler.
I'll try to make her sing.

The Oda Nobunaga Type

Oda was a superb military strategist who brought peace to Japan in the age of warring states. His strategy was to get to his enemies before they could get to him.
The silent bush warbler.
Let us shoot it down
Before it can sing.

● The Office Layout

Office layouts differ by company, but these represent the most typical patterns.

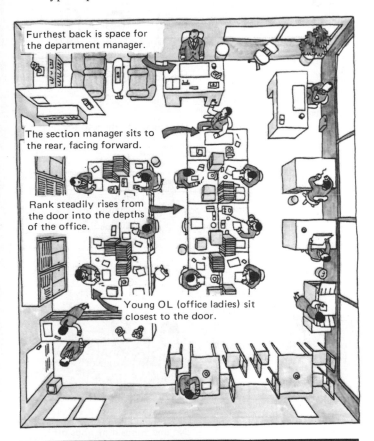

Furthest back is space for the department manager.

The section manager sits to the rear, facing forward.

Rank steadily rises from the door into the depths of the office.

Young OL (office ladies) sit closest to the door.

● Recognizing the Highest Ranked

His business card will generally be presented by a subordinate. Sometimes he will not even carry a card.

He sits the farthest to the rear.

He drinks his tea first.

He speaks the least.

He speaks last.

No one minds if he nods off.

● Recognizing Rank by Car Manners

The highest ranked used to sit deepest in the back seat.

More recently, he rides where it is easiest to get in and out.

When the owner is driving, the **highest ranked sits in the passenger's seat.**

If the owner's wife is along, she sits in the passenger's seat.

Climbing stairs, the highest ranked walks last.

Coming down, he walks first.

HIGH-TECHNOLOGY JAPANESE COMPANIES AND PRODUCTS

There are some interesting contrasts between high-technology businesses in Japan and, for example, those in the United States. One that immediately comes to mind is the difference in the rates at which new products appear on the market. The domestic Japanese market for consumer electronics products like stereos, televisions, personal computers, video players and the like is even more ferociously competitive than the export market, as a result, new models, with new features and (often minor) variations on old ones, appear on the market at a truly dizzying pace, many of them destined to survive for only a matter of weeks or months if sales don't measure up in comparison to the competition.

Another particularly noticeable difference has to do with job mobility. The supposedly traditional Japanese pattern of "lifetime employment" has been disappearing steadily during the postwar period; only about one third of Japanese workers today can expect to spend most of their working lives working for a single company. But the rate at which highly-trained engineers and technicians change jobs in Silicon Valley, often once every 2 to 3 years, would seem almost inconceivable to their Japanese counterparts. Even though the mobility of such highly skilled professionals in Japan is higher than for other types of workers, they change jobs far less frequently than their American counterparts.

William Raike (U.S.A) Editor

THE LIFESTYLE OF SALARYMEN

サラリーマンの生活

●

For the salarymen, even their private
life is centered around and dominated by the company.
Let's take a look at their family life, amusements,
joys and worries.

COMPANY DORMITORY

Most large Japanese companies maintain residences for their employees *(Shainryō)*. Sometimes, single houses or sections of apartment complexes will be rented, while dormitories designed to hold over 100 employees and family members are very common.

Some dormitories are equipped with tennis courts, gymnasiums, and other recreational facilities.

Many have playgrounds for the children. A salaryman and his family who live in such a dorm may come to rely upon the company for almost every aspect of their daily lives.

Company dormitories are divided into singles and family types. The singles dorms will have a cafeteria where breakfast and dinner can be served at extremely low prices.

Family life at a company dormitory has many courtesies and customs which differ from normal conditions.

It is common for wives to act in accordance with their husband's rank at the office whether it be bragging or acting with excessive humility. Wifely jealousy directed toward the spouse of an elite employee sometime results in domestic quarrels. Being salarymen is not always easy!

Japanese salarymen dream of owning their own homes, and nothing could be worse than spending one's whole life in a company dorm. Most salarymen hope to purchase a home around the age of 40 and strive with their wives to put aside every yen possible.

Within the dorm, wives of higher ranked employees assume the leadership, often forming "circle" groups. Refusing to join such circles will damage the husband's chances of promotion, and many wives participate grudgingly.

Family trips for dormitory residents are very common. Step by step, a salaryman learns to consider his own free time in terms of the company.

COMPANY TRIPS

Company trips are often held for the employees of a certain department or section. Family members rarely join such excursions, and because the trip is meant to strengthen group solidarity, refusing to participate is frowned upon.

The destinations are usually hot springs or other tourist spots. Many Younger salarymen now choose to pass up these company excursions.

Company trips are based on group activities. Participants assemble at the station at a set time, then ride in the same train car to the destination. Oftentimes a bus will be rented for the transportation.

The days are dominated by golf, tennis, hiking and other invigorating sports.

Nights are reserved for dinner parties. A large room is rented out for eating and drinking, with many employees unveiling their *kakushigei* (hidden talent) for singing, comedy, etc.

In April, company groups gather for *hanami* (flower viewing). Drinking parties are held in parks under the cherry blossoms *(sakura)*, with singing and generally boisterous activity often lasting until late at night. These parties are an important event which help mark the arrival of spring.

Lodges and other company-owned resorts are often used for outings. These facilities are also available for individual use by employees and their families.

運動会

SPORTS DAY

In October, most companies hold large-scale *undōkai* with as many as 1,000 or more employees and their families participating in friendly sports competition. Much like company trips, the sports day is considered a method of boosting employee unity and morale.

Each cheering section is clearly marked by its own uniform and flag.

Top managers view the competition from special seats.

The company is divided by plant, branch, or department, with different sections competing against each other. With the honor of their section at stake, everyone goes all out to win.

Wives and children bring box lunches and compete as well. The result is enhanced unity extending to employee families as well.

Female employees form the cheering sections. Chosen are the youngest and prettiest, who strive to put on a good show to compare favorably with other sections.

The most popular events include

Tsunahiki (Tug-of-war)

Bōtaoshi (Pole-fighting)

Kibasen (Piggy-back headband grabbing)

BŌNENKAI/SHINNENKAI

In December and January, each company section holds two major parties. December brings *bōnenkai* ("forget-the-year parties" held to close out the old year), followed in January by *shinnenkai* ("New Year's parties" held to ring in the new year). Both are key events which are attended by all employees.

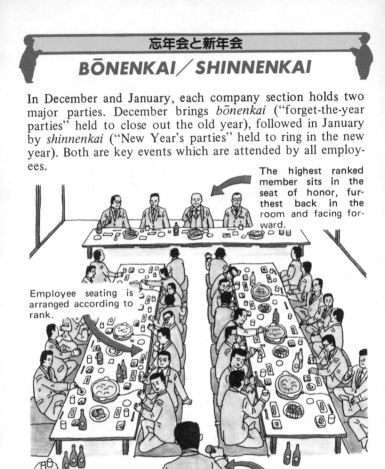

The highest ranked member sits in the seat of honor, furthest back in the room and facing forward.

Employee seating is arranged according to rank.

The front area is used for the stage and presentations of *kakushigei*.

All salarymen practice for such occasions, hoping that their *kakushigei* will please and impress their superiors.

The most orthodox *kakushigei* is *karaoké* (singing along with taped music). However, just singing well is not enough, clever choreography and other touches are needed to make a truly memorable impression.

Some employees use traditional dancing or musical instruments to put on a good show.

While the parties are informal in principle, excessive drunkenness and picking fights with one's superior can result in minus points when work resumes the next morning.

Books are published to guide those who lack confidence in their party talents.

CLUB ACTIVITIES

Companies offer many different clubs, with employees usually belonging to at least one or more. Circle activities take place at company facilities, and the company helps pay the bill. In this way, employees come to spend much of their private time at the company as well.

Clubs are both cultural and sports oriented. Cultural types offer computer lessons and other training which will be of practical use on the job. The most popular sports circle is baseball.

Salarymen who belong to several such circles come to regard the company as the genuine focus of their lifestyle.

Salarymen in their 20s usually belong to a sports circle and try hard to impress female co-workers or jobsite superiors.

Salarymen in their 30s get married and start families, and their busy work schedules allow little time for circle activities.

Salarymen in their 40s take computer programming or other classes in the efforts to attain new knowledge and skills. They are constantly discouraged by the gaps between themselves and younger employees.

Salarymen in their 50s turn to *haiku, bonsai* or other traditional arts. Many have begun to sense their own human limitations and use these pursuits to fill the emptiness they feel with regard to everyday life.

SCHOOL CLIQUES

Some companies are dominated by managers who are graduates from the same university. At such firms, only those from specific schools can expect to gain meaningful promotions. At companies with several different *gakubatsu*, there is often intense competition to produce top managers from one's own alma mater.

Leading *gakubatsu* schools include Tokyo University (*Akamon*), Waseda University (*Tōmon*) and *Keiō-gijuku* University (*Mita*).

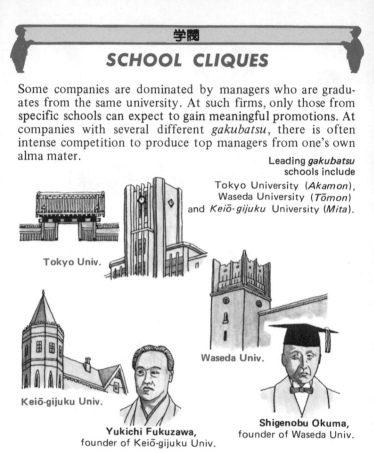

Tokyo Univ.

Waseda Univ.

Keiō-gijuku Univ.

Yukichi Fukuzawa, founder of Keiō-gijuku Univ.

Shigenobu Okuma, founder of Waseda Univ.

Company *gakubatsu* are normally quite exclusive, and parents fear that if their children do not attend the "right" university they will never succeed in life. The result has been fierce entrance examination competition to enter the "best" schools, although there is a more recent trend to favor individual ability over academic background.

"SAME YEAR GROUP"

The *dōkikai* is a group of employees who entered the company in the same year, regardless of what section they belong to. Members hold parties and go on trips together, with their activities serving to strengthen solidarity on a level separate from the actual company organization.

The *dōkikai* is a custom with origins in the old Japanese military, in which those entering the service in the same year became good friends and helped each other out.

While members feel close to those in the group, they are also rivals in the competition to achieve. Consequently, while there is certainly cooperation, there is also no shortage of attempts to trip up a rival's efforts to climb the corporate ladder.

The *dōkikai* also organize trips, sports days, year's end and New Year's parties, and other gatherings apart from the company organization. One result is a further toll of a salaryman's holiday and free time.

社内結婚

INTER-COMPANY MARRIAGE

Shanai Kekkon refers to marriage between a couple who both work at the same company and is a very popular pattern in Japan. The large number of such marriages is a reflection of the nature of life within Japanese companies.

Because of their work and company-related events, the young salarymen have little private time to speak of.

The majority of female employees enter the company between the age of 18 to 20 upon graduation from high school or junior college. Their schedules also permit little private time.

A female employee marrying the son of an executive will be assured of a rosy future. This is referred to as *tamanokoshi* (climbing onto a jeweled palanquin — i.e., marrying into money).

Most female employees marry within three or five years after entering the company, upon which they resign. This is known as *koshikaké* (a seat, or stepping stone). The company is like a temporary seat for these women, who leave to be replaced by others, who will also be gone in a few years.

WORKING COUPLES

Recently there has been a rise in the number of households with working couples. Both husband and wife attend to jobs held outside of the home.

If they have no children, some-times they are called "DINKS" (Double Income No Kids).

When there are small children, the working couple also have the task of taking their children to the nurs-ery school as well as leaving the company early enough to pick them up.

There are also many working couples who share the responsibil-ity of doing the housework.

Since the organization of Japa-nese society still has not changed, increasingly the burden of solving children's problems and maintain-ing neighborhood relations has fallen on the working wife.

When there are no children, or the children are grown and out on their own, the lifestyle of a salaryman's wife is extremely monotonous. She will encounter many dangers and temptations as a result.

6:30 a.m.
The wife begins to fix her husband breakfast.

Midnight
The tired hubby arrives home, and she lays out his bedding.

During the day, she sits frozen before the TV.

When there are no children in the home, the wife's work consists of these two basic chores. Between these jobs, she has little to do and spends much of her time alone, inside the home.

She will take many approaches to break the monotony.

One of the most common solutions is to join housewives with the same dilemma for shopping or for gab sessions over tea.

Outgoing wives play tennis, golf or other active sports. Such behavior was rarely seen up to just a few years ago.

One of the wife's duties is to shuttle the kids back and forth to school by car or on foot.

When the husband is rarely at home, the wife and children take off to amusement parks or movies together.

A SALARYMAN'S HOLIDAYS

While Japanese salarymen are indeed hard workers, they naturally do have holidays. Nevertheless, they often find it very difficult to use this free time for private pursuits.

Work

Holidays are often considered one phase of work. An extremely common example is golf with company superiors or clients.

Home

Because salarymen have little chance for daily contact with their families, they often feel compelled to go to amusement parks or the zoo on holidays. This is known as "family service" (*kazoku sābisu*) in Japan.

Recuperation

Exhausted by their work, many salarymen use holidays to catch up on sleep. Such holidays will consist largely of napping, television and meals.

Figuring eight days off per month, a common pattern might be:

The first Saturday of the month:
Play golf with superior.

The first Sunday:
Exhausted from golf, sleep all day.

The second Saturday:
Report to the company for holiday work.

The second Sunday:
Take family to the local zoo.

The third Saturday:
Day trip with co-workers.

The third Sunday:
Company baseball tournament.

The fourth Saturday:
Attend a co-worker's wedding.

The fourth Sunday:
Entertain client during a round of golf.

NEW YEAR'S DAY

A salaryman enjoys three major vacation seasons during the year — summer, winter, and the "Golden Week" period in late April to early May. New Year's *(Shōgatsu)* is the single most important event in Japan, and most people return to their home towns to ring it in.

Expressways are backed up for kilometer after kilometer.

The *Shinkansen* Bullet Train is packed to over 300 percent capacity.

Commuter trains are empty.

Deep lines form in airport terminals.

The standard company New Year's vacation runs from around December 28 to January 5, depending on the calendar for that year. About 80 percent of salarymen living in greater Tokyo form a huge exodus to their home towns, jamming all modes of transportation to the prefectures.

Although salarymen go to great pains to make it home to the countryside, they often find it impossible to relax and enjoy there.

Otoshidama

The children of relatives and friends expect to receive *otoshidama* (New Year's money) of 500 to 3,000 yen from every adult in sight. Sometimes 20 or more kids will show up during the week, creating a real drain on a salaryman's already flimsy budget.

Nenshimawari

Nenshimawari (New Year's calls) is the custom of donning full traditional dress and calling on company superiors or other persons to whom one is indebted. By the time ten or more of these calls are performed, *Shōgatsu* may be nearly over.

Hatsumōdé/Hatsuhinodé

Shōgatsu is the first day of the new year, and immediately after midnight, many Japanese travel to shrines for *hatsumōdé* ("first worship") or stay up all night to pay reverence to the rising sun (*"hatsuhinodé"*) in the morning. New Year's resolutions are popular although easily forgotten.

The salaryman becomes exhausted toward the end of this vacation and sleeps all day long. Without this bit of rest, he will find it tough to weather the packed conditions on the way home.

ALL SOUL'S DAY

Bon falls on July 15 according to Japan's old calendar, and on August 15 in the modern calendar. People again return to their home towns, pay respects to their family graves, and then wait at home for the souls of their diseased ancestors to arrive.

Water is sprinkled on the grave-stone. Fresh cut flowers are carefully placed, and incense sticks are lit.

Graves are generally located near the home of the male head of the family (father, grandfather, etc.) Salaryman must thereby fight the crowds to get home, just as they do for *shōgatsu*.

At night the family gathers with relatives to eat and drink and strengthen their bonds and hopes for future health and prosperity.

With the focus on *Bon*, company summer vacations last for a week to ten days. Some people choose pleasure trips instead of the grueling trip home.

OL (office ladies) who commute to work from home have much more time and money on their hands, and many enjoy overseas trips once or twice a year.

Young salarymen scrimp and save to be able to marry the OL of their dreams. Some take no summer vacations at all, stay in their dorm rooms or apartments, and subsist on instant *rāmen*.

Middle-aged salarymen take their families on trips. Unfortunately, the tourist spots are jammed at this time of year, transforming the pleasure trip into an exhausting struggle.

Naturally, some salarymen choose to work right through the summer vacation season.

ゴールデンウィーク
"GOLDEN WEEK"

Four national holidays are concentrated in the period from late April to early May. Adding in Saturdays, Sundays and a day or two of paid vacation time, it is possible to take off for a week or more. This period is known as "Golden Week" in Japan and ranks as the third most popular vacation season after *Shōgatsu* and *Bon*.

Vacationers flock to local tourist spots during Golden Week. In the Tokyo area, Tokyo Disneyland and Ueno Zoo are two of the biggest draws.

The national holidays are the Greenery day (April 29), Constitution Day (May 3) and Children's Day (May 5). Salarymen who don't put in for time off in advance may end up at work between holidays. (May 4 also was recently designated a national holiday to encourage more Japanese to vacation and relax.)

OLs normally commute from their parent's home, eat a home-made lunch or a cheap meal at the employee's cafeteria, and have their way paid by superiors when they go out drinking at night. In other words, they are able to bank most of their paychecks, allowing them to take elegant vacations compared to salarymen.

They wear leading fashion brands and dine on high quality French cuisine.

They enjoy golf, tennis, and other sports which cost big money to play in Japan.

They are more than willing to use every day of paid vacation time to take off on trips.

Male employees always pay for meals, further swelling OL bank accounts.

中元と歳暮
MID-YEAR AND YEAR-END PRESENTS

Twice a year, Japanese send presents to person they feel indebted to. In July it is the *chūgen* ("midyear present") and in December it is the *seibo* ("year-end present"). Department store sales peak during these two periods.

Some salarymen must send to several dozen persons, while receiving few if any presents of their own. This shopping may eat up half of their bonus

Executives commonly receive gifts from over 100 or more persons and are forced to turn an entire room into a gift storehouse.

Popular presents include soy sauce, cooking oil and other long-lasting food products, tableware, towels, soap sets, etc. The result is piles of the same basic items, which cannot possibly all be put to practical use.

For those who have received a large number of presents, writing "Thank You" cards turns out to be quite a considerable chore.

Unusable presents can be exchanged at department stores for gift coupons of the same value.

Some presents are given to the neighbors, others sold at bazaars.

Executives receiving large amounts of *chūgen* (midyear presents) often lose track of who gave them what.

WEDDING AND FUNERAL CEREMONIES

Kankon Sōsai means wedding and funeral ceremonies. The salaryman's world is rooted in human relations, and attending co-workers marriages or funerals is considered mandatory. These ceremonies are expensive and provide another drain on the salaryman's budget.

Both have been drinking, and only the color of their neckties tells them apart.

Smells of incense.

Carrying a large bundle of presents.

Buddhist rosary beans

Traditional dress for weddings is a black formal suit and white necktie. Salarymen returning from a wedding can be easily recognized by this attire and by the large bundle of presents (*hikidemono*) they carry.

Dress for funerals is the same black formal suit worn at weddings but a black necktie. This is very convenient, and it is possible to attend both a wedding and funeral on the same day by simply changing ties.

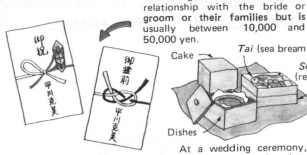

The cash gift is determined by the relationship with the bride or groom or their families but is usually between 10,000 and 50,000 yen.

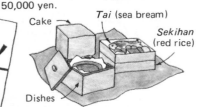

Cake

Tai (sea bream)

Sekihan (red rice)

Dishes

Persons attending weddings or funerals bring cash gifts. The money is placed in a *noshibukuro* (a special formal envelop) bearing the character for "congratulations" (weddings) or "prayer" (funerals).

At a wedding ceremony, guests receive presents close in value to the cash expected to be received. These are known as *hikidemono*. No such custom is practiced at funerals because of the considerable economic burden on the bereaved family.

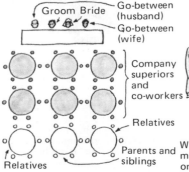

Groom Bride — Go-between (husband)
Go-between (wife)

Company superiors and co-workers

Relatives

Parents and siblings

Relatives

The majority of wedding guests are usually co-workers or other company relations of the bride and groom. A superior will often act as the *nakōdo* (official go-between) for the couple.

受付

When a key member of a salaryman's family passes on, his subordinates assist with the funeral preparations. A superior will always attend the funeral of a company man, with telegrams containing messages of condolence sent from the president or other executives.

AMUSEMENT 1 PACHINKO

Pachinko is a game of chance indigenous to Japan. "*Pachinko* parlors" are found in the vicinity of almost any train station around the country, and the game is one of the favorite recreations of salarymen.

"Lucky Seven"

A combination of the *pachinko* and slot machine concept for enhanced gambling excitement. When all three digits stop on seven, the gate opens up and about 5,000 yen worth of balls flood out.

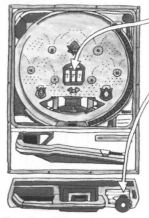

Today almost all *pachinko* machines are electric, with the balls flipped up automatically by turning a knob. The 100 yen worth of balls will be exhausted in only 10 seconds or so, meaning that a considerable investment may be required to find a machine that pays off.

To play, 100 yen is paid for a couple dozen steel balls, which are poured into a chosen machine. The balls are flipped up to the top of the vertical pinball-like machine, and some fall into holes to win extra balls. Accumulated balls can be traded in for various prizes at a special counter.

About one-third of a parlor's machines are reset on a daily basis. Gamblers try to find machines which paid off the previous day and have not been reset. Often lines will form in front of the parlors before they open in the morning.

The prize corners resemble small supermarkets, offering items ranging from cigarettes, stationery items and books, to fruits, vegetables and underwear.

A salaryman intending to relax in a *pachinko* parlor for a few minutes during his lunch break will sometimes become so absorbed in the metal balls that he squanders away all his pocket money. He may even be late reporting back to the office.

Picking up balls which have fallen to the floor is considered unlucky, not to mention cheap!

AMUSEMENT 2　MAHJONG

Mahjong ranks with *pachinko* as a game highly popular with salarymen. Four players sit at a table and strive to combine 108 tiles containing three suits of numbers and 28 tiles with *kanji* characters into set patterns.

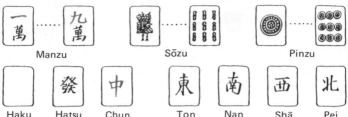

Manzu　　　　　　　　Sōzu　　　　　　　　Pinzu

Haku　　Hatsu　　Chun　　　Ton　　Nan　　Shā　　Pei

All start with 13 tiles, then draw and discard to build four sets of three and one set of two identical tiles.

Points are awarded according to the difficulty of the sets. Although against the law, these points are normally computed into money, with payoffs made at the end.

AMUSEMENT 3 HORSE RACING

There are four types of legal gambling in Japan — horse racing, bicycle racing, speedboat racing and motorcycle racing. Horse racing is the most popular and ranks as a favorite past time for many salarymen.

Three typical type track visitors

The baseball cap and sunglasses type. This is a popular style for professional gamblers or horse racing freaks.

The polo shirt, golf slacks and silver rimmed glasses type. Most salarymen lean toward this look.

The jeans, sneaker and sweatshirt type. A style often adopted by poor college students who want spending money or simply enjoy the sport.

127

AMUSEMENT 4 OTHERS

In Japan, where parks and fields are scarce, the amusements of salarymen are often confined to the indoors. They have no time for travel and have recently been consumed by the craze for "FAMI-CONS".

(1) FAMI-CON

Fami-con is a computer game software for home CRT use. Adults as well as children, have become obcessed with these games.

(2) Baseball

Even though it is called "baseball", we are referring to a game of "catch" played on rooftops and back alleys in park-scarce Japan. Regardless of the conditions, Salarymen love baseball.

(3) Disco

Disco is popular with the young salarymen. Pathos surrounds the site of the salarymen dancing in their suits and ties.

Business and Religion

Japan's religions are Shinto and Buddhism, but it is very rare for these religions to directly influence business practices. Yet, when new offices are opened or construction starts, religious rituals are observed. Also, when the administrator happens to have a religious orientation personel and even company policies may be determined by the ordinations of the gods.

This is a purification ritual praying for the prosperity of the company or business during the opening of a new office.

The green branches are for good luck, the *"maneki neko"* cat beckons customers and money and the daruma's eye is colored in when a wish is granted. All are seen in the offices of service industries.

The alter piece – *Kamidana* – is often found in the president's office. The presidents will always bow to it before departing. This is and individualistic ritual to help one spiritually focus on their work.

129

A SALARYMAN'S JOYS AND ANXIETIES

Unlike many reports, Japanese salarymen are not happy-go-lucky economic warriors crazy about every aspect of their work. They are normal human beings, with normal joys and anxieties.

Promotion and success within the company are a salaryman's greatest joys.

Tasting the sadness of life upon a demotion transfer (see page 48).

Closing a business deal or completing a project brings distinction.

When work doesn't go well, stress builds up.

The bonus — a favorite of any salaried worker.

Receiving a bonus is nice, but the other guy always seems to get more.

Commendation — Receiving the "president's award," "ingenuity prize," "salesman of the year," or other honors is naturally an occasion for joy.

No matter how hard he tries, things just don't go as they should.

SALARYMAN BLUES

Middle-aged salarymen must juggle many problems, originating both at work and at home. Here we examine a few typical examples.

Bullying
The news has been filled lately with incidents of children being physically and mentally bullied by classmates. Many suicides have resulted.

Physical punishment
Some teachers resort to physical means to discipline students, which sometimes become violent.

Delinquency
Juvenile delinquency has also struck Japan, with some children skipping school, joining motorcycle gangs, drinking, sniffing glue, and causing other trouble.

Refusing to go to School
Some children become neurotic and refuse to attend school.

Education
Children's education is a critical concern in Japan.

Wife's Unfaithfulness

After the kids, a salaryman's greatest worry is usually his wife. When there is little husband-wife communication, the chances of the wife cheating on the side are multiplied.

His Own Unfaithfulness

Some salarymen carry on with a young OL at the company, a situation known as "office love." Few have banked enough money to possibly afford the divorce and alimony that this behavior could **lead to and go to great lengths to** keep the affair secret.

Taking Care of the Parents

It is normal for the eldest son to take care of his parents until the end. If the old folks grow senile or sickly, this can be a huge drain on his savings and his wife's time and strength.

Home Loan

The majority of salarymen take out 30 to 40 year loans when they purchase a home. The payments are often like a ball and chain in their daily lifestyle.

REASONS SALARYMAN WANT TO QUIT

Japanese salarymen are extremely diligent workers. However, most will think of giving up their lifestyle at least once during their career. A survey by the Prime Minister's Office revealed the following reasons for this desire to throw in the towel.

1. Not enough pay
Salary is found to be insufficient to cover children's schooling, make the home loan payments, and handle other financial demands.

2. Can't put knowledge to work
An engineer, for example, finds himself spending his entire day working a pocket calculator.

3. No freedom
Constant pestering from superiors to do things differently.

4. Long working hours
Physical exhaustion from day after day of overtime.

ストレス解消法
METHODS OF ALLEVIATING STRESS

Salarymen work hard and are confronted with stress on a daily basis. The following are stress alleviation methods compiled from a survey by a leading Japanese business magazine.

1. Grin and bear it
The Japanese are often said to be less than skillful at recreation and other means of personal enjoyment. The same is true of stress, with many salarymen choosing to simply hang on and endure.

2. Sports
Young salarymen work out their frustrations on the tennis court or baseball diamond, while middle-aged salarymen enjoy golfing.

3. Reading
One of the handiest methods is to lose oneself in a comic book or mystery novel.

4. Open up to a confidant
Being able to talk about problems to trustworthy superiors, colleagues, or friends is very important.

THE SALARYMAN'S HEALTH

In their 20s and 30s, salarymen work to the limits of their physical stamina, often relieving the stress with alcohol. When they suddenly begin to run out of steam in their 40s, they at last become concerned with their health.

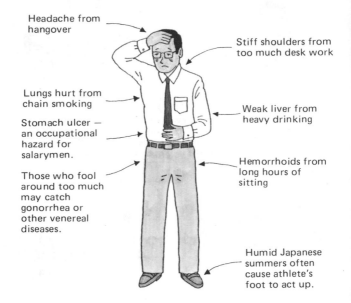

Headache from hangover

Stiff shoulders from too much desk work

Lungs hurt from chain smoking

Weak liver from heavy drinking

Stomach ulcer — an occupational hazard for salarymen.

Those who fool around too much may catch gonorrhea or other venereal diseases.

Hemorrhoids from long hours of sitting

Humid Japanese summers often cause athlete's foot to act up.

The most common salarymen ailment is the nervous stomach ulcer. Because of the frequency of such ulcers, most companies view them on the same level as the common cold.

Salarymen suffer from lack of sleep and hangovers, rarely exercise, eat irregularly, have a poor nutritional balance, and are usually chain smokers. In short, it is a miracle they are alive at all.

Salarymen attempt to improve their health with the following methods.

Peppermint-flavored pipes are used by those trying to give up smoking.

Anti-smoking

Most salarymen try to stop smoking but rarely last for more than several days. As a result, imitation cigarettes, chewing gum, special candy and other anti-smoking aids sell well in Japan.

Jogging

Influenced by America, jogging has caught on in Japan. There is some doubt, however, whether jogging in the heavy exhaust emissions of Tokyo is all that good for the health.

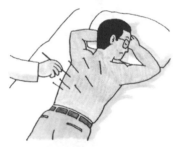

Oriental Medicine

Japan is experiencing a resurgence in the popularity of oriental medicine. Many salarymen place their faith in acupuncture, moxibustion, massages and other Eastern approaches.

Many layman's cancer preventatives have been publicized. Many kinds of herb medicines are sold in drug stores.

REQUIRED READING FOR SALARYMAN

The Japanese are avid readers. Many books target salarymen, presenting new knowledge and skills geared to help them succeed in life and work.

Because salarymen don't have much time for serious reading, they devise unique techniques.

By far, the most common is reading on the train, which has led to the overwhelming popularity of pocket-size books.

Coffee shops are widely used for meetings or business talks. Some salarymen arrive early to catch up on their newspaper or book reading.

Some buy books they have no time to read and end up gathering dust on their desks.

Others carry their books into the bathroom.

Books or magazines preferred by salarymen include the following.

Weekly Magazine Pictorials

Thin magazines specializing in photos and short comments on the latest hot news and scandal. These magazines sell around 2.5 million copies per week.

Salaryman Magazines

Targeting young salarymen, these magazines explain how to succeed at the company and sell about one million copies per week.

History

Middle-aged managers often study history to learn how famous generals from centuries ago commanded their armies and fiefs. Sometimes, the lessons are applied to the coaching of baseball, with subordinates organized into winning teams.

Salaryman Novels

Extremely numerous, these novels adopt the salaryman lifestyle as background. Some tell of high-powered management success in big companies, although those which delve into the highs and lows of middle managers are the most popular.

THE SALARYMAN SPIRIT

Magazines dealing exclusively with the secrets of salaryman life and success are unique to Japan. Typical know-how presented in these publications includes ....

To succeed at work, a salaryman must be able to adapt mentally, physically and spiritually. Spiritual adaptation is directly dependent on the ability to get along with fellow workers and other persons. To master the art of skillful human relations, it is useful to notice what kind of persons attract others.

Persons who are good at listening

Persons who never verbalize their complaints or insult others

Persons who always manage to look on the bright side of life

Be liked by your boss!

A salaryman's fate rides on the impression he leaves on his direct superiors. Proper treatment, seasonal presents and other service to superiors is a must to get ahead.

Your Superiors Must be Successful!

Flattering will get a salaryman nowhere if his superior is a *mado-giwazoku*. Becoming the subordinate of an elite superior is important for future promotion.

Collect In-House Information!

The human relations at big companies are complex. Early attainment of reliable personnel information can put a salaryman in an advantageous position. One effective method is to get on good terms with an executive's secretary and milk her for the latest news.

Know How to Play!

A successful salaryman must be skillful both at work and play. Golf, mahjong and other games, for example, are important for customer entertainment. He should also avoid dating women from the same company, sticking to professionals or those with no ties to the company.

MIDDLE CLASS

When asked if they are upper, middle and lower class, 90 percent of Japanese reply middle class *(Chūryū)*, while some 70 percent of this total regard themselves as upper middle class. This uniformity of income and lifestyle level is a dominating characteristic of Japanese society.

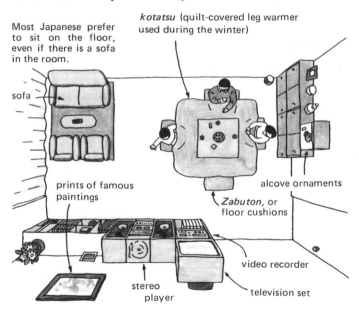

Most Japanese prefer to sit on the floor, even if there is a sofa in the room.

kotatsu (quilt-covered leg warmer used during the winter)

sofa

prints of famous paintings

alcove ornaments

Zabuton, or floor cushions

video recorder

stereo player

television set

The typical middle-class home consists of five room blocks — the living room, bedroom, study, children's room and bathroom (including bath and toilet). Home parties are rare in Japan, with the living room normally used to entertain guests or other visitors.

● Prerequisites for a Middle-Class Lifestyle

Japanese consider themselves middle class under the following conditions.

Owning their own home. Unfortunately, the exorbitant land prices in Tokyo and other large cities force salarymen to settle for apartments or rental homes, while most retreat to the distant suburbs.

Owning a four door sedan.

Owning a complete set of golf clubs.

Their children attend private preparatory schools (*juku*) to train for college, senior or junior high school entrance exams.

Take a trip once every six months or so.

Eat out with the family at least once a month.

THE BUSINESSMAN VS. THE SALARYMAN

No matter how many similarities they appear to have, the Japanese salaryman is completely different from the American businessman.

It is true that on the surface they appear identical but my experience in a Japanese company convinced me otherwise. Probably the most basic difference lies in attitudes towards work. In Japan, the average working man centers his life around work. Overtime is not uncommon and most afterhours friendships start at the workplace. Personal life is secondary at best.

Americans, on the other hand, value their personal lives at least as much as their jobs. There are, of course, workaholics in every country, and different professions have different demands, but Americans usually stick to a straight 9 to 5 schedule.

The fact that the salaryman spends more time working does not necessarily mean that he works more than his American counterpart, however. The seniority system and job security in Japan provide little incentive to work efficiently and overtime is often nothing more than a front for the benefit of superiors.

Rampant sexual discrimination and a host of other problems led to my decision to work freelance but the issue of personal time was to me, the one thing I could not adapt to.

We work to live, not live to work.

Martha Chaiklin (U.S.A) Translator

THE MANNERS OF SALARYMEN
サラリーマンのマナー

●

Japan's business world has its own unique manners.
It has its own conventions, all of which developed
from close ties with Japanese culture and history.

敬語

HONORIFIC LANGUAGE

The existence of an honorific level of speech makes Japanese an extremely complex language. *Keigo* consists of *sonkeigo* (terms of respect) and *kenjōgo* (terms of condescension), with several levels in each category. Skillful use at this level is difficult even for the Japanese.

Greetings When Calling Upon Someone

Familiar: (With a slight wave) *"Yaa"* ("How ya' doing?").

Polite: (Bowing slightly) *"Konnichiwa"* ("Good afternoon" or "Good day").

Keigo: (Bowing deeply) *"Ojama shimasu"* ("Please excuse intrusion").

Saying Goodbye

Familiar: (With a slight wave) *"Jyā-né"* ("Be seeing you").

Polite: (Bowing slightly) *"Sayōnara"* ("Good bye").

Keigo: (Bowing deeply) *"Shitsurei itashimashita"* ("I'm sorry to have disturbed you").

● How to Use Keigo

Good morning!

I'm so sorry!

As a general rule, *keigo* should be used when the other person is older. If that person speaks in the familiar language, it is permissible to drop to the "polite" form. Use of *keigo* to a younger person, however, can sound sarcastic.

Keigo is also used to address those in higher positions. For salarymen, the criterion is company post. Furthermore, position takes precedence over age, making it permissible for a 30 year old *kachō* (section manager) to "speak down" to a 40 year old *kakarichō* (chief clerk).

Please give us your business ....

How about a drink tonight?

Subcontractors also address clients from big companies in *keigo*. Company size and sponsorship are more important than position, and the president of a small or medium-size company will often address the *kachō* of a big company in *keigo*.

When both parties are convinced they are equal in position, they use *keigo* in the beginning and drop to "polite" language from the second time on. If they get on well, they may drop down to the familiar language.

MANNERS AND TABOOS

Japanese culture is filled with ritual, and specific words and gestures often have deep meaning. As a result, complicated behavioral standards tend to dominate wedding and funeral ceremonies. Salarymen must follow many manners and taboos in daily life.

● **Greetings**

Office colleagues or subordinates are greeted while walking with a wave of the hand and "*Ossu*," "*Yaa*" or other greetings.

Those slightly higher in rank (*kakarichō, kachō*, etc.) are also greeted on the move with a slight bow of the head.

Those much higher in rank (*buchō*, etc.) are greeted after stopping with a slight bow. Bowing too deeply in such chance meetings can look foolish.

● Greetings on Tatami Mats

On tatami, one should bow in the formal upright seated position.

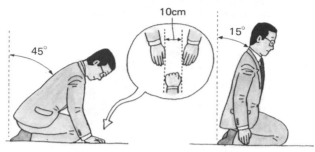

Truly formal tatami greetings are performed by stretching the upper body forward 20—30 centimeters, placing the hands on the mat about one fist apart.

For abbreviated greetings, touch the fingers to the mat on either side, and bow slightly forward.

It is impolite to lift the face or keep the hands stuffed in one's pockets during such greetings.

It is also unbecoming to touch the head to the mat or curl one's back while bowing.

● On The Train

The worst possible experience on a rush hour train is to be accused of being a masher. With no way to move, the victim must endure the insulting stares of other passengers, until he can slip off the train at the next station.

When the packed conditions make it impossible not to touch a woman, make sure it is with the back of the hand. Touching with the palm leaves little grounds for excuse.

The safest possible posture is to cling to a strap with one hand and read a book or newspaper with the other.

It is very poor manners to open up a newspaper on a crowded train.

Most trains have "Silver Seats" for the elderly and handicapped. While it is not absolutely taboo for others to use these seats during rush hour, it demonstrates a clear lack of propriety.

● Presents

In addition to *chūgen* and *seibo*, there are plenty of other situations in which gifts are considered necessary.

There is an unwritten rule that a salaryman on a business trip must bring back local specialities for his co-workers. Since the company is considered one big family, this practice resembles a father bringing home goodies for the kids.

The custom of presents for those at the company also extends to private trips taken on private time.

Giri-choko

For hospital visits, never take a potted flower. Since the flower will not wither *(nezuku)*, it will be interpreted as a sign of extended hospitalization.

On Valentine's Day, Japanese women give chocolates to their boyfriends. At the company, however, it is often expected that young OL give their superiors *giri choko* ("duty-bound chocolates").

151

● Manners When Visiting

When visiting a Japanese home, the shoes are removed at the entryway.

The shoes should then be placed together at the edge of the entrance, pointing outward. Salarymen arrange the shoes of any superiors they are with.

When visiting someone in a more senior position, the host will come out to greet the visitor and will then open the door to let the visitor enter first. Forcing a more senior person to enter first is considered rude.

Do not sit directly on the floor cushion. First sit on the right, then move quietly toward the cushion. Greetings are performed off the cushion.

● How to Sit in a Japanese-style Room

Toko-no-ma

Toko-no-ma

doorway

In a formal Japanese-style room, the *tokonoma* (an alcove with a hanging scroll and other decorations) faces the entrance. Persons in a superior position sit by the *tokonoma* in the seat of honor, and subordinates sit near the entrance.

In newer buildings, the *tokonoma* and entrance may flank each other. If so, the seat of honor is located as far from the entrance as possible, offering a good view of the garden or the room itself.

● How to Sit in a Western-style Room

In a Western-style room, the sofa is the seat of honor and armchairs the lower seats. The guest naturally sits on the sofa.

Putting your feet up on a desk in a Japanese company is definitely not acceptable behavior.

● Japanese Table Manners

Table manners for Japanese cuisine are complicated and few people really understand the official methods. An understanding of basic etiquette is sufficient to avoid embarrassment on most occasions.

How to Pick up Hashi (Chopsticks)

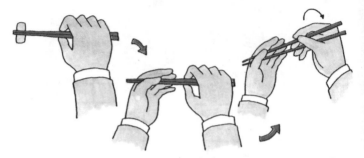

Pick them up in the right hand.

Cradle them with the left hand.

Adjust the right hand grasp to eat.

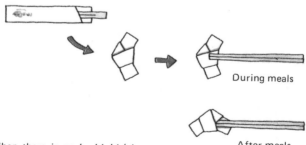

During meals

After meals

When there is no *hashioki* (chopstick stand) for wooden *hashi*, use the paper container as the rest.

● Avoid the Following Mistakes

Zuborabashi
Holding the chopsticks and bowl in the same hand.

Yosebashi
Moving a bowl with the chopsticks.

Tsukibashi
Skewering food with the chopsticks.

Mayoibashi
Hovering over the table with chopsticks poised, pondering what to eat.

Saguribashi
Digging through a common dish of food to locate a tasty morsel.

Inugui
Eating while leaning over the plate like a dog (*Inu*).

● Eating Japanese Food

Mastering *hashi* (chopsticks) will allow you to enjoy Japanese food with no major trouble. However, learning a few basic manners will help deepen your understanding of Japanese culture, and good etiquette will create a favorable impression on those around you.

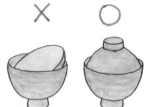

When a bowl contains a lid, remove it and place it upside down on the table. When the bowl is on an *ozen* (tray for Japanese cuisine), place the lid alongside the tray.

When finished, replace the lid on the bowl, in its original position, not upside down.

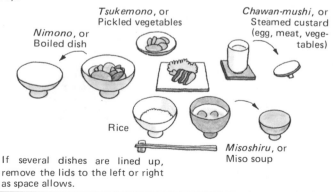

Nimono, or Boiled dish

Tsukemono, or Pickled vegetables

Chawan-mushi, or Steamed custard (egg, meat, vegetables)

Rice

Misoshiru, or Miso soup

If several dishes are lined up, remove the lids to the left or right as space allows.

● How to Eat Sushi

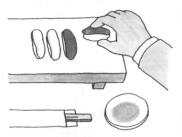

Normal customer   Rich man

Sushi is one of the most popular Japanese foods. It is usually eaten with chopsticks, but if you have trouble it is quite acceptable to pick up the individual pieces by hand.

After one is accustomed to eating at sushi restaurants, newcomers to a shop are eager to sit at the counter to order from a wide variety of items just to savor the shops' specialties. But in this case, it's really hard to figure out just how much to pay the first time. Therefore, it's a good idea to go along with a habitué of the restaurant to get a fair deal.

● How to Eat Soba (Noodles)

Master

Another favorite food is *soba* (noodles). The most acceptable way to eat *zaru-soba* (cold buckwheat noodles) is to grasp small portions of the noodles with the **chopsticks and noisily suck them** up into the mouth. However, few people, including the Japanese, ever master this special art.

Although most *soba* shops are similar, a clear distinction is drawn between high-class and popular-class establishments. While customers at the high-class shops are intent on savoring their *soba*, in the popular-class shops they lounge around reading comic books, sports newspapers or other publications.

● Funeral Manners

While wedding manners are not very complicated, not knowing how to act at funerals can be uncomfortable. Japanese funerals are conducted in either Buddhist or *Shintō* style.

Buddhist Style

Buddhist funerals feature *shōkō*, a ceremony in which incense is offered to the soul of the departed.

Hand-clapping is a taboo.

First, bow slightly.

Holding *juzu*, a string of rosary-like beads, the hands are clasped and the eyes closed for prayer.

A pinch of powdered incense is touched to the forehead and then placed in the incense burner as an offering.

Then the hands are again clasped around the *juzu* and another prayer offered.

Shinto Style

In a Shintō-style funeral, an offering of *sakaki* leaves is placed at the altar.

The mourner receives the leaves.

They are touched to the forehead.

The branch is pointed outward, then turned 90 degrees.

Change hands, then turn the branch 180 degrees until it is pointed toward oneself.

Place the *sakaki* leaves on the altar and perform a 90-degree bow.

Clap twice quietly.

A final 90-degree bow.

EXPATRIATES LOOK AT SALARYMEN

OPENING OF JAPANESE MARKET

Usually, under the pretense of opening Japan's doors to imports, Japanese companies ask the Government to revise their standards to fit the products they buy from foreign countries or produce abroad. After that, it is anounced that, for the good of foreign exporters, some standards have been revised. Then, if you have a foreign-made product, you think that, finally, you will be able to sell your goods in Japan, instead of having them bought by the Japanese in your own country, where they use and abuse the export incentives your country offers.

However, you'll be probably wrong, besides never being sure whether your goods will pass through customs or not, as there is always one more regulation. Therefore, in order to avoid such trouble, you have to get some firm information from the organs concerned which usually are established in big buildings in central Tokyo. At first, you ask the receptionist on what floor you can obtain the information needed. After laughing a bit because you are a foreigner, she tell you to go to the 7th floor, room 707, for instance. You go up, enter a room full of files, and beyond them there are some Japanese reading or talking on the phone. One by one, they all look at you, and finally the lowest-ranked one comes to train his English on you. After a while, someone tells you to go to the 11th floor, and there you hear that you could get the information you need on the 4th floor of the annex building. By the end you have entertained some 69 people.

If you don't understand the Japanese language, that is still all right because you think that all of them just tried to be nice to you, although incompetent. Let's say that you find some Japanese official in Kobe that tells you there should be no trouble to import your product. After that, at the time your goods arrive to Japan, you find out that that person has been transferred to a distant place. His substitute is a completely new thing, and deals with your case depending on how he spent last night. And, he can always find a stone to put in your way. If you don't have an influential Japanese on your side, because bribery is not accepted in Japan, you have to   send your goods back home.

Paulo Berwanger (Brazil) Importer

BUSINESS RELATED
PHRASES AND TERMINOLOGY
ビジネス用語集・ビジネスに関連した用語と語法

●

There are a number of special business
terms in Japan, let's introduce those basic terms most
often encountered.

AMBIGUOUS BUSINESS VOCABULARY

Japanese people have a tendency to avoid saying a distinct yes or no. Here are some words with meanings that change with the situation.

Hai

Hai is one of the hardest words for non-Japanese to grasp. It generally means "I see," while as "yes," it is normally used to emphasis agreement, a pledge to carry through on something, and so forth. Accordingly, failing to confirm the real intention of "*hai*" can invite unexpected misunderstandings.

Iié

While *hai* means "yes," *iié* usually means a simple "no," although under certain circumstances *iié* can also mean *hai*, further complicating things.

It is considered polite to say *iié* upon receiving a present, even though the item will be accepted.

Japanese will say *iié* when they have been praised, even if they're sure they deserve it.

Dōmo

This is a prefix used in front of "thank you," "I'm sorry," "good bye," "how are you" and other expressions. *Dōmo* has developed into an extremely versatile word which, even when used alone, can signify any of these expressions. In this sense, it is the single handiest word in the Japanese language.

Ah, dōmo

present

Offering a light expression of gratitude.

dōmo   *dōmo*

When meeting people, *dōmo* can be used in place of both *konnichi-wa* ("hello" or "good day") or *sayōnara* ("goodbye").

Sumimasen

One of the most widely used expressions in Japanese. It is widely thought to mean "I'm sorry," and can also be used to offer a light expression of gratitude.

Ah, sumimasen

It is also useful in restaurants or coffee shops to get the attention of a waiter or waitress.

Dōmo sumimasen

The combination of *"Dōmo-sumimasen"* is the most popular way to express stronger apology or thanks.

Zensho-shimasu, Kentō-shimasu, and *Mata renraku shimasu* are ambiguous expressions used to reply to a business request. They each have a between-the-lines meaning that is different from the literal one.

Yoroshiku

This is an expression often used when requesting assistance or co-operation. It is generally utilized as a ceremonial nuance, meaning "I'm counting on you" or "Please lend me your strength."

A)

Zensho-Shimasu

Literally, means "I will do my best to meet your wishes." However, it can also be used in the context of "I may try hard, or maybe I won't"; or, "I'll try if I feel like it." This leaves little room for complaint if someone says *zensho-shimasu* and then does nothing.

B)

Kentō-Shimasu

In Japan, it is considered impolite to say "no" directly. *Kentō-shimasu* carries the nuance "We need some time to study your proposal" but is fairly negative in nature. Rather than a flat out no, the feeling is "I'll think about it, so please leave." Again, it is difficult to complain if no further developments result.

C)

Mata Renraku Shimasu

"We'll contact you later," means much the same as *kentō-shimasu* and thus can be used to inflect "no." In that case, the sense is "I may get in contact if I feel like it," and naturally no lie has been told if no phone call is ever made. A much more positive nuance is provided by saying "I'll contact you within a week," or "Please contact me."

Shitauké & Magouké

"*Shita*" means under, while "*uke*" means to receive. It refers to work done under a prime contractor — the sub-contractor. **"*Mago*"** means grandchild, and "*Magouke*" refers to sub-sub-contractors. The existence of sub-contractors and sub-sub-contractors is a special characteristic of Japanese industry. The tremendous growth in Japanese industry is said to stem from these sub-contractors bearing most of the economic risks.

Arubaito & Pāto

Both terms refer to part-time jobs. *Arubaito* is from the German "arbeit". "*Baito*" is also used as an abbreviated form. Generally, both terms refer to student's part-time jobs.

Shokutaku & Shukkō

"*Shokutaku*" refers to non-regular employees, while the act of going to work at another company for a specific job is called "*Shukkō*".

The 3 systems of part-time jobs, the sub-contracting, and non-regular employment are keys to Japanese enterprises ability to cope with fluctuations in the market.

Hei-sha & On-sha

In the business world, the use of honorific terms are necessary. One's own company is called the *Hei-sha*, while other's companies are called *On-sha* or *Ki-sha*.

Hidari-uchiwa

"*Hidari*" means left (hand) and "*uchiwa*" is a fan. In Japan it has the meaning of one who holds a fan in their left hand; in other words, it is someone who doesn't work hard and lives the easy life. It refers to very good working conditions.

Ishin-Denshin

It is a zen term describing the process of expressing one's thoughts to another directly, without the use of words. Using *Ishin-denshin* instead of contracts in conducting business is said to be the "Japanese way of business."

Kotsu

The original meaning of "*kotsu*" was bone. It has evolved into meaning "the essence," "conditions" and "knack" of how to do things. It appears in expressions as "He finally has grasped the "*kotsu*" of business." "*Kotsu*" is not something studied through theories but learned through experience.

Haburi

"Ha" means "a bird's wings," while *"buri"* is "to swing."

It has come to refer to social prestige and popularity. *"Haburi ga yoi"* (good haburi) means that business is going well and is prospering.

Tantō Chokunyū

The literal translation is "a sword enters directly." It refers to being direct and saying exactly what one thinks.

The Recent Trend of Abbreviating and Changing Everything into Japanese

It is often the case that when foreign words are adapted into the Japanese language they are abbreviated, making them easier to pronounce. For example, an *"Ofu-kon"* refers to an office computer. These abbreviated words have created a boom of sorts. Here are a few samples:

Paso-kon: A personal computer.
It is said that the personal computer, along with the "fami-kon" (family computer) using game software has created a new era.

Maza-kon: A mother complex.
The number of salarymen with this complex has increased in recent years.

Wā-puro: A word processor.

OA & FA: Office automation and factory automation. Both trends are going to change Japanese business tremendously.

TERMS RELATED TO THE HUMAN BODY

The Japanese language has a large number of terms relating to the human body. As an example, *"Te"* (hands), or *"Mi"* (body) are used as metaphors to express a variety of meanings. A traditional way of thinking exists, stemming from the apprenticeship system in which work is seen as being learned not through theories, but through one's hands and bodies.

Té

Of all the body related terms, the hand terms are the most numerous, the majority of them being business related expressions.
In Japanese, *"Te"* can mean "hand," "arm," and "palm".

(1) Té o someru

Its meaning is to start work on a project.

(2) Té ni amaru
"An amount so great it won't stay on one's palm" is the direct translation. It is used to indicate that one is in a situation beyond one's control.

(3) Té o yogosu
"To dirty one's hand."
Its meaning is to get involved in "dirty" work.

(4) Té o utsu
"Put one's hands together and clap."
It is used when reaching agreement in business talk or negotiation.

(5) Té o mawasu
"To extend one's hands."
It is used to indicate using a variety of measures to devise a counter-plan.

(6) Té o nuku
Ténuki
"Pull out one's hands"
It means to skimp on something one has to do (to skimp on one's work).

(7) Té o hiku
"To pull back ones hands."
It means to stop doing something. In other words, to withdraw from a project.

(8) Té o hirogeru
"To extend one's arms wide open."
It means to expand one's business to increase one's equipment and provisions.

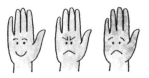

(9) Yoi té, Warui té, Kitanai té
"good hand", "bad hand" and "dirty hand," respectively. They mean a good method, an inferior method, and a vicious method.

Ashi

Ashi – foot or leg
It often means money and is a word essential to business.

(1) Oashi
Even today, merchants use this word to mean money.

(2) Ashi ga deru
"The foot that was hidden slipped out."
It means to go in the red.

(3) Ashi o hipparu
"To pull someone's leg."
It means to interfere with someone's promotions or success.

(4) Agé ashi o toru
"To take the leg in the air and cause someone to fall over."
It means to reproach someone for a slip of the tongue.

(5) Ashi ga chi ni tsukanai
"One's feet don't reach the ground."
It means not to be realistic or someone who is not soberminded.

(6) Ashi ga hayai
"To run fast"
It has come to mean that product sales are good.
It can also mean that food is easily spoiled.

Mi

It means "self", "body", and "mind".
Along with these three meanings, it also has an extremely deep meaning. This word is one of the more difficult for westerners to understand.

(1) Mi ga katamaru
"One's 'self' becomes fixed."
It means for one's position to stabilize. "*Mi o katameru*" means to get married.

(2) Mi ga hairu
　　Mi o ireru
"To put one's heart into it."
It means to give it one's best shot and try his hardest.

(3) Mi ni tsuku
"Something attached to oneself"
It means knowledge or techniques that have been mastered.

172

(4) Mi o tateru
"To stand one's body up."
It means to succeed or advance.

(5) Mi o kudaku, Mi o kezuru, Mi o ko ni suru
In order, the literal meanings are (1) to crush one's body, (2) to pare down one's body, and (3) to make one's body into powder. The meaning is (1) to do one's utmost, (2) very painful, and (3) to work very hard.

Hara

Literally stomach, but in this case it's closer to "heart" or "mind".

(1) Hara o waru
"Opening up" one's mind, saying what one thinks.

(2) Hara guroi
Literally, "black hearted."
Refers to schemers who hide their real intentions behind sweet-sounding words.

(3) Haragei
"Performing from the heart." The ability to tailor strategy and tactics to particular situations and triumph in business talks or negotiations largely on the strength of one's personality.

(4) Hara ni ichimotsu aru
"Having something in one's heart." In other words, harboring an ulterior motive.

Literally, one's waist or hips.
The *"koshi"* is at the center of one's body. The term is used of relating to the martial arts.

(1) Koshi ga hikui
"A low waist."
It means modesty or humility.

(2) Koshi ga kudakeru ▷
"A broken waist."
In the process of attempting to complete something, it means that he has failed to complete the project.

BUSINESS SEEN IN PROVERBS

Tsuru no hitokoé

The literal meaning is "a voice of a crane."

It refers to a word of command from one's lord. A single word from the company president is often "the voice of a crane". What he says becomes law.

Nō aru taka wa tsumé o kakusu

The literal translation is that smart hawks hide their claws. It has the same meaning as the saying "still waters run deep".

Ishi no ué nimo sannen

The literal meaning is that if one sits on a rock for 3 years, it will heat up. It has the nuance that if one is patient and perseveres, one will succeed. It is the same as "Perseverence brings success".

Saru mo kikara ochiru

The literal meaning is that even monkeys fall from trees. It has the same meaning as "Even Homer sometimes nods", and "Even the best have their failures."

A SALARYMAN'S GESTURES

Japanese words can have various meanings. In companies which do not permit extensive individual authority, salarymen will often intentionally use ambiguous expressions during business talks. To grasp someone's real intentions, it is thus important to observe specific gestures and all other sources of data.

Saying *koré* (this) and forming the OK sign with the thumb and index finger means "money talk."

Pressing the index finger to one's lips means "we can't discuss that here."

Waving one's hand before one's own face is an extremely strong refusal.

Folding the arms and closing the eyes is a sign for, "Be quiet, I'm thinking it over!"

● Warai (The Smile)

The Japanese smile can mean many different things.

Positive Smile
Japanese smile when they like or agree with someone.

Negative Smile
Smiling immediately after a statement can signal a light denial or a joke.

Smile of Denial
Sometimes Japanese will smile when they don't want to respond to a question. This is the same as saying "no comment."

Stoic Smile
A smile when upset with someone's attitude and unable, for various reasons, to express this in words.

Smile of Apology
Smiling in hopes of being forgiven.

Smile of Confirmation
Smiling to learn what the other person thinks of your opinion.

● Gestures of Salarymen

Scratching the head is a way of hiding confusion or embarrassment.

One indicates oneself by placing the extended index finger on the tip of one's nose.

When calling someone towards you, you place the palm down and wave your hand up and down. This should never be done towards a guest or superior. It would be considered rude.

With both the thumb and index finger extended, gesturing drinking means "let's go drinking".

Holding a clenched fist in front of the face in imitation of a long nose implies that the person under discussion is, like the long-nosed goblin "*Tengu*", a conceited braggart.

When passing in front of people, excuse yourself by stooping slightly and holding out the hand with the edge downwards as if you are cutting your way through.

Holding up the index fingers like horns on either side of the forehead indicates that a third person (perhaps a boss or wife) is angry.

The gesture of pretending to cut off the head means "to be fired."

Touching the index fingers together like swords clashing indicates that people are quarrelling.

Holding a clenched fist beside the head and suddenly opening the fingers expresses the opinion that a person is "pā" (stupid or crazy).

The thumb can mean "father", "the boss" or a "superior", while the baby finger signifies a secret woman friend other than one's wife.

POSTSCRIPT

A Word About Japanese Management and the "Salaryman"

The economic surge of postwar Japan, notably the achievements of the companies behind this growth, continues to startle the world. Japan's GNP is now No. 2 in the free world, while its overseas assets rank at top global levels. As a result, Japan is now the target of more criticism and envy than ever before. Trade friction with the West, for example, at press time was reaching yet a new peak. Japan, meanwhile, has yet to mobilize a policy capable of rapid improvements in the trade imbalance.

On its darker side, this situation has led to harsh criticism of Japanese workers as "economic animals" or "workaholics." On a brighter note, many Western scholars are voicing keen interest in the Japanese style of management.

Why is a nation both criticized and praised for what it has achieved? Is Japanese economic competence in fact the result of Japanese-style management? Do foreign impressions of the Japanese "company" accurately reflect the true state of affairs? To answer these and other questions, it is vital to delve closely into the daily lives of the workers and managers grouped under the broad category of "salaryman." This book does just that, and seeks to communicate the feelings, systems and specific

activities of the "economic warriors" who continue to keep Japanese business on the move.

●

Is "Japanese-style management" superior to its overseas counterparts? Until recently, Westerners were fond of pointing out that the "seniority system," "lifetime employment," the "bottom-up decision-making mechanism" and other systems as inherent weaknesses in the Japanese company. This interpretation has generally resulted from close attention paid to the recent prowess of light electric appliances, computers, light automobiles, service and other high-growth fields. These sectors have risen in the wake of the decline of heavy industry, brought on by demand slumps in the steel, heavy electric machinery, construction and other fields which grew on the strength of these traditional systems.

There is no conjecture, however, regarding Japan's startling progress in the four decades following defeat in World War II, rising quickly to join the ranks of the economic superpowers. Japan has successfully dealt with the impact of two oil crises and global stagflation, managing to maintain economic growth at the five percent level throughout.

Uncovering the secret of this "oriental magic" is no easy task. Western scholars, particularly those in the United States, have searched for answers in Japan's cultural characteristics, Japanese-style management strategy, the diligence of her people and other social factors. Some have gone so far as to

call the situation the defeat of the rationalized management approach taught in American business schools. While none of these theories are totally off the mark, the Japanese themselves find some fairly humorous. This is because the Japanese have been the world's most eager students of Western-style management and have put these methods to active use in their own industrial pursuit.

Closer examination of the Japanese company reveals that it is nearly impossible to identify any fixed approach which can be neatly summarized as "Japanese management."

More plausible is the concept that "excellent companies have no national boundaries." From a different perspective, this means that "Honda," "Mitsubishi" and other corporate groups can hardly be said to share totally identical cultural characteristics simply because they are both Japanese in nationality.

Nevertheless, a total view of Japanese corporate society does reveal a certain consistent trend. Most Japanese will have at least a general (if not sometimes vague) understanding of this trend.

Ask any Japanese what has supported their nation's postwar economic prosperity, and the most likely reply will be, "the salaryman." The so-called "salaryman" is clearly the key word in unraveling the factors behind this unprecedented 40 year economic rise.

The core of Japan's economy does not consist of the sophisticated strategies of special "excellent companies," nor

of systems in which the public and private sectors join hands to advance government-promoted projects. This core consists simply of the "salaryman," nothing more, nothing less. These salarymen range from employees of huge companies affiliated with the financial combines *(zaibatsu)* of the prewar era, to the men who work at small cottage industry factories. Their ranks reach from veteran war generation salaryman, to young economic warriors still wet behind the ears. But without the devoted efforts of all salaryman over the years, Japan's current prosperity would be only a pipe dream, if that.

In a very real sense, the word "salaryman" is synonymous with "the driving force of postwar Japanese economic growth."

●

There is no single term which expresses the true meaning of "salaryman." Literally speaking, it might be said to refer to the "salaried worker," although this would mean that almost all workers in Japan could be defined as "salarymen." This is incorrect, however, because salaried workers such as retailers, those employed by tiny companies, and those in education, medicine, religion or other fields are not normally referred to as "salarymen." Perhaps the English word closest to the "salaryman" concept is "white collar," referring most specifically to workers employed by Japanese *shosha* (trading companies) or assigned to the home office of large or medium size companies. Yet even this does not begin to cover the entire sphere of salaryman activity.

The large Japanese company is a society within a society, governed by a strong sense of family solidarity. The president is the father, and the employees are the children. Prime contractors, subcontractors, sub-subcontractors, sub-sub-subcontractors and other companies are also included in the extended family ranks, even if they do not enjoy capital affiliation. This is a society in which honor and loyalty carry far greater weight and significance than any signed contract.

Viewed from the rational Western view of business, the Japanese approach might seem to be filled with waste and strain. However, a closer look reveals no shortage of positive elements within this family-like organization, which operates largely on the basis of tacit understanding and trust.

Let's take a typical example. An American newly hired by a Japanese company is ordered by his superior to serve coffee. The American refuses. "There is nothing in my labor contract about serving coffee," he insists. "If such chores are also to be part of my job, I expect to be paid extra for them."

In Japan, an order from a superior is considered the command from one's father, whether any mention of specific conditions is made in a labor contract or not. It is important to understand, however, that a superior will often make up for unreasonable orders by treating his subordinates to a few drinks after work, many times paid for out of his own pocket money.

One more example: Mr. A from a subcontractor is visiting the materials department of the prime contractor's plant for business talks. The negotiations are suddenly interrupted, as the entire company halts work to participate in the 3:00 p.m. radio calisthenics. Looking around, Mr. A sees that other outside visitors are taking part in the exercises, and he joins in, too. There are many examples like this, in which the policies and activities of the client (prime contractor) penetrate down through employees of subcontractors as well.

What many non-Japanese find particularly difficult to grasp is that these examples do not stem from carefully stipulated standards. Rather, they are part of a silently understood and spontaneously accepted code. Simply stated, Japanese companies have successfully incorporated the remnants of the binding traditions and rules of communal village society into modern management methods. Even so, this deep-rooted corporate society is gradually being pushed toward change, eroded by remarkable shifts in the industrial structure from the mid-1980s, and the influence of the increasing number of young Japanese reared in Japan's highly Westernized postwar culture. Today the generation gap is one of Japan's most pressing social problems and is touched upon in this volume where it is relevant to the main theme.

●

This book zeroes in on the true face of the "salaryman," offering the reader rare access to the inner workings of Japanese corporate society. Because of space and stylistic considerations, we have avoided any technical analysis or evaluation of the Japanese management approach. Rather, the emphasis is on characterization of the typical "salaryman lifestyle," with parody used in many cases.

Some readers will claim that all salarymen do not fit the pattern presented in this book. We would respond that our objective was not to stereotype, but to increase general understanding of the overall "salaryman" concept, while providing insight into the world of Japanese business. We also believe a need exists to explode the popular myth that all salarymen are happy business warriors, dedicated first and foremost to forwarding the interests of Japan, Incorporated.

●

In preparing "SALARYMAN" IN JAPAN, we held discussions with a broad range of salarymen, ranging from major manufacturing concerns and trading houses, to small and medium scale companies. These encounters left us with a strong conviction that the "salaryman society" is a realm possessing its own special rules and ethics, much like the worlds of political or student life in Japan. There are many cases in which the thoughts and actions of salaryman are rooted more strongly in the traditions and conventions of their

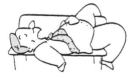

company than in the tenets of general human behavior. In view of the diverse realm of persons who comprise this segment of society, from employees of huge companies to those of tiny cottage industry operations, from the technocrat to the door-to-door salesman, this is an extremely unique phenomenon.

There are any number of theories which explain why such a diverse range of people can be grouped together under the common "salaryman spirit" heading. Perhaps the old standby — "oriental magic" — may have something to do with it after all. We do nothing more than present the facts and leave the ultimate verdict on this and other questions to you, the reader.

Finally, we wish to extend our sincere gratitude to the many "salarymen" who so generously shared their time and thought with the members of our staff. Without their candor and cooperation, this book would never have made it to press.

INDEX

英文 日本絵とき事典 8

ILLUSTRATED
"SALARYMAN" IN JAPAN

初 版 発 行	1986年12月10日
改 訂 7 版	1996年1月1日
	(Jan. 1, 1996 7th edition)
編 集 人	藤嶋良二
発 行 人	岩田光正
発 行 所	JTB 日本交通公社出版事業局
印 刷 所	交通印刷株式会社

著 者	平川克美
企画・編集	JTB 出版事業局 編集二部
	外語図書編集 担当編集長 谷羽美紀
取材・編集協力	株式会社アーバン・トランスレーション
イ ラ ス ト	松下正己
表紙デザイン	東 芳純
翻 訳	Dick Belcher

●図書のご注文は
JTB 出版販売センター ☎03-3477-9588
〒150 東京都渋谷区道玄坂1-10-8 渋谷野村ビル7階
●本書の内容のお問合せは
JTB 出版事業局 編集二部 ☎03-3477-9566
〒150 東京都渋谷区道玄坂1-10-8 渋谷野村ビル7階
●広告のお問合せは
JTB出版事業局 広告部 ☎03-3477-9566

954312 712102
ISBN4-533-00665-5